SELECTED POEMS

SELECTED POEMS

Ruth Fainlight

including
2 libretti
and translations from
Jean Joubert
and
Sophia de Mello Breyner

SINCLAIR-STEVENSON

First published in Great Britain in 1995
by Sinclair-Stevenson
an imprint of Reed Consumer Books Ltd
Michelin House, 81 Fulham Road, London SW3 6RB
and Auckland, Melbourne, Singapore and Toronto

A CIP catalogue record for this book
is available at the British Library

ISBN 1 85619 569 4

Typeset by Deltatype Ltd, Ellesmere Port, Cheshire
Printed and bound in Great Britain
by Cox & Wyman Ltd, Reading

CONTENTS

Translations

**from: MARINE ROSE, Selected Poems, Black Swan Books,
Redding Ridge, CT, USA, 1988.**
'The Islands' first appeared as the English section of a
trilingual edition (Portuguese, French, English) of
NAVIGATIONS, Imprensa Nacional, Casa da Moeda,
Lisbon 1983.

from: CINQUANTE TOILES POUR UN ESPACE BLANC,
Grasset 1982; LES VINGT-CINQ HEURES DU JOUR,
Grasset 1987; LA MAIN DE FEU, Grasset 1993;
and uncollected poems printed in JEAN JOUBERT par
Michel Cosem (collection 'Visages de ce temps' dirigee par
Jean Digot), Editions du Rouergue, Rodez 1994.

PREFACE

This is an enlarged version of *Selected Poems*, 1987, to which have been added poems from my 1990 collection, *The Knot*, translations from the work of the Portuguese poet Sophia de Mello Breyner and the French poet Jean Joubert, and the texts of two libretti written for the Royal Opera House's *Garden Venture*.

Though I appreciate the arguments of those who believe that a poem should be left in its first published state, I feel that the relationship between poet and poem, like a living marriage, is continually changing, and so have taken the opportunity to revise some of the work. As in any relationship, it is impossible to know if one's actions will have good or bad results.

RF

from

Cages, 1966

DAWN CHORUS

There comes a moment when the tide turns:
Light has won again. The birds stop singing
For a long moment, then begin again
On a more casual note. They've done it:
Dragged back day, tipped cool light
Over the lock of dawn with the nervous force
Of their throats. Some strength of mine
Was sapped to bring that toneless even glare
And settle the question: after each dawn's
Struggle, in the clear white of exhaustion,
Insomniacs float down wide canals of sleep.

THE ANGELS

They're poised like statues, civil, dignified,
Interested even, as photos on tombstones are
By a stranger who peers curiously.
The soil is stony, friable. Dry roots break
As I clutch out to stop my downward slide
Into the pit, the place they're solemnly
Admiring. Why don't I cry for help? They seem
So courteous. One would surely bend
From his shallow ledge, reach out a hand.
But my tongue stays still as the empty sky,
As their faces in the stern unwavering light.

THE INFANTICIDE

I left my baby there among the trees,
Rain-rusted leaves, decayed stalks,
Twigs husked with grey and white moss.
The black mulch makes a soft bed.
Perhaps he will not cry, lulled
Till I am far enough away
By sky's dazzle, the touch of ferns and air.
From the top of the woods I hear nothing.
Silence is like a plastic sheet over
His stretched mouth, stifling his thin alarm,
Powerless to stop the mist.
I left my baby there among the trees
And now the frogs can have their will of me.

EQUINOX

More than a week of storms —
Storms and sickness —
Between now and my last clear view of the moon.

In two more nights she'll be full.
Thunder, bruised clouds, a sea like melted stone,
Confirm her waxing arrogance.

Full moon had no such heralds through the summer,
Nights of stars, moon discreet somewhere
In all that glitter. Now the stars have no chance.

This is her season of power, she is everywhere.
The wind scoops mock moons,
White crescents of waves on the violent water.

Three times magnified, she flashes through streaming
Cloud like a wrecker's beacon.
Her lurid halo makes the sky seem hollow.

Time is slowed by storms — more will happen
Before she gains full circle than between
One full moon and the next in calm weather.

from

To See the Matter Clearly, 1968

THE SPIRIT MOVING ON THE
FACE OF THE WATERS

At first it seems to flow forward.
But sea's as rooted as a wheatfield,
Slides from crest to trough forever,
Heaves its shining mass
But never throws the rider.

Suspended in the bowl of continents,
Ocean dreams of margin,
Nirvana of dissolution,
Spray flung onto stone,
The heavenly beaches of evaporation.

Waves goad the water
With the shape of freedom.

GLORIA

However she's personified
Or represented,
I won't forget
How space expands
Until it can include
A million goddesses and concepts.

Sophia, Anima, or Kali,
White or black, death or wisdom,
The central fire
Or all-engulfing water,

My muse is in myself:
As past and future
Only exist
By my own need to think them,
This power is manifest
In her resplendent figure.

She makes me dance,
She frightens me at night
With horrors,
Leads me to the burning-place.

She stands behind the mountains
Like the sun,
And lifts her arms to show
That they are flesh,
That all this valley is alive
Because she wills it so.

TO SEE THE MATTER CLEARLY

Through reason's telescope the figures
Seem distinct and small.
A jeweller's precision must have
Formed the cunning limbs, instilled
The counterfeit of feeling that
Articulates those manikins.
Their piping voices barely reach
The ear, and eye is strained by such
Elaborate enamelling,
The play of each expressive feature.
It's easy, though, to change the focus,
Be overwhelmed by giant agony:
Huge soft pitted faces mouthing
Pain, and clumsy yearning gestures.
Shift glass again, turn down the sound,
Retreat to that high vantage point
And leave them thrashing in the undergrowth
That through the telescope
Shines beautiful as jewels.

SLEEP-LEARNING

All that I try to save him from
Is what he dreams about.
I watch his face
Each night emerging clearer,
Stern son who reads my dreams:
The dreams I had
And those my brother had
And which my parents learned from theirs,
Moving behind mauve lids
That seal his eyes.

He dreams I want to leave him,
Roams through night forests, desolate.
And I dream I've abandoned him:
First punish, then atone.
Next morning both our faces
Mark the change:
Mine with the guilty look of those
Who knowingly succumb to dreams,
And his the gaze
Of someone learning.

FEVER HOSPITAL

The fever pustules first appear
in creases and the hidden parts.
The war is far away, I am safe here.
I sit at home. I live where there is peace.
My child plays submarines and guns
Though I discourage him. But every day
He senses what I read in the newspapers.
Perhaps he knows more than I do.
He trains himself for his expected future.

The fever symptoms break in me
As fascination with destructiveness.
I watch those whom I think my opposites,
Ignore complexities, and let them act
What I am too fastidious
To execute myself: those drenching
Surges of maliciousness, the dreams
Of torture (though I disinfect
My fantasy by playing victim).

If I must purge myself of fever
By surrogates: the monkey-man,
The Fascist, the monopolist, even
The householder and his dull omissions,
I spread the sickness just as much.
I mould the world as if I pressed
My form into a bed of wax
And called that shape my opposite;
As if external evil makes me good.
The country is at peace, at least I claim
That I am, though my dreams are troubled.

My child imagines dangers everywhere,
Demands to know the natural weapons
Of each creature, its protection.
For he was born into this fever hospital
And learns geography to make quite sure
Just where the tanks and airplanes are
Enacting the realities of power
Which I try to disclaim. It is no good.
The fever breeds within my blood.
This hectic flush must signal quarantine
To every corner of the universe.

NIGHT MARE

I shut the moon behind the door:
Bathroom floor so light I could not sleep
So I had closed the moon away.
But she was straining
And the door was creaking.

Alone in bed I felt so cold.
Full moon in winter's coldest time
And you had gone away. Full moon
Was my love's enemy
And I was cold with fear.

Naked behind the door, black hair
Around her head like branches
Of a winter tree, white body
Full and glistening,
The night mare waited,
Pawed the shining tiles and waited,
Menacing, and silently.

WIDE-EYED

Blind chance, blind fate,
Blind destiny, blind guides,
Blind paths and alleys.
Blind hope and blind malevolence.
Blind faith. Blind Justice
Clutching at her scales.
Blind love. Wide-eyed jealousy.

UNCERTAIN

Because I talk about my life with you
With you, that changes it. You say I want
Approval, totally. It must be true
That viewing matter changes it. The patterns
Shift as if responding to disturbance.
What I learned from Heisenberg is true:
Viewing matter changes it. Results
Cannot be modified, controlled, predicted.

The mechanism which I once set up
For watching me with you, to magnify
All motives, analyse each thought and action,
Has made the wounds I'm bleeding through.
Examining one's life is sure to change it,
And I'm exhausted by this repetition
Of a lesson I already knew:
Once change begins, everything's uncertain.

from

The Region's Violence, 1973

LILITH

Lilith, Adam's first companion,
Assumed her equality.
For this she was banished.

God had created her
From the same earth as Adam.
She stood her ground, amazed
By the idea of differences.

Adam and God were embarrassed,
Humiliated. It was true —
They had been formed
At the same time, the two
Halves of His reflection.

Her expectations
Should have seemed justified.
But Adam needed to understand God.
A creature must now worship him,
Constrained and resentful as he.
God encouraged him.

To guard His mystery, God
Made Adam swoon.
There, when he awoke,
Awaited Eve, the chattel.

Eyes downcast, his phallus
The first thing she noticed.
The snake reminded her of it.

That nagging ache in his side
Where the rib was extracted
(In memory of which
The soldier thrust his spear)
Keeps Adam irritable.

Lilith's disgrace thus defined
Good and evil. She would be
Outside, the feared, the alien,
Hungry and dangerous.
His seed and Eve's fruit
At hazard from her rage.

Good wives wear amulets
Against her, to protect themselves.
Lilith is jealous.

FIRE-QUEEN

Unseen, snow slides from over-laden boughs.
Spume of flakes, flurry of light, cold smoke;
Kaleidoscope of crystal and lead and flame.
Then silence again as it sinks,
Weightless, lost, white into whiteness, down
To permafrost encasing molten turbulence.

That core answers the sun-spots, flares
When her impotence most torments – she
With her presumptions and gestures, who has chosen
This place rather than any other
To expose herself to the gnawing ulcer
Of her own nature. Such is her kingdom,

Fire-queen of the absolute north,
Who rules by satire, inertia, disdain;
Touch blunted to ice, ears sealed,
Sight gone, reflection congealed, mirror
Shattered aeons ago, rather than see
Merely a pattern of line and colour, flat

As the diagram of what a face might be –
Which to recognize would mean to accept
The clamour of voices, imploring, complaining,
But silent, that rise from her brain like steam
From a tubful of churning laundry.
But silent. Her thoughts: unspoken, ignored.

Their heat is the power that freezes, motor
Of her repression-machine, refrigerator
Of frightful patience, rigid mastodon-throne,
Sealed and invisible ice-pyramid,
Red-hot iron maiden of self-hatred
She's trapped inside by refusing to listen.

23

Screams settle like snow and never thaw.
Branches petrified under their burden
Of murdered desires. She sits like Lot's wife,
Ambitionless as death, perfect, absorbed
Forever by her silent incantation,
Beyond the need for sanction, or praise.

SNOW POEM

      birds stream over the houses opposite
I watch from my window
      one veers, passes through glass as if it were smoke
settles on my table

      it is snowing
      I stare at whirling flakes with such intensity
they drift into the room
transform it to a paperweight

      snow covers my papers
      the bird prints patterns with his feet
hieroglyphs appropriating
what I've written

      the bird flies up   one flake
approaches, huge, revealing
its precision and its symmetry
before it muffles me

SILENCE

When you ask for consolation
From one of them, burnt children
Who were never loved – or so
The explanation runs –
They do not understand. Perhaps,
Like speech, it is a skill
Which must be learned at its specific
Moment. Once past, nothing
Yet known can activate
That latent aptitude.
The child remains both deaf and dumb.
The one you turned toward –
A loud, gesticulating mute.

How they torment, who always
Must retreat, as if attacked
By such demands, whose last defence
Becomes exposure of a pain
They moan and rage is fiercer far
Than yours. Heart-broken, you muffle
Your own complaint, adjusting
To the region's violence,
Leaving grief abused, unspoken –
Until, beyond the reefs
Of hopelessness, nothing seems lacking
In this solitude. You've grown
Accustomed to the silence.

PIGEONS AT VILLA BELMONTE

After he mounted her, wings
Fluttering with joy of domination,
Neck iridescent with coppery
Lombardy green and the terra-
Cotta of the Villa Belmonte (she
Smaller, darker, reserved, the same
Grey surrounding the shutters),
She strutted onto his neck as if
In casual imitation, hopped off,
Then up and down, across, a few more
Times. They bent their heads towards
Each other, seemed affectionate,
Their burbling cries conjugal.

I've read that pigeons, caged and left,
Will pluck each other bare and bleeding.
That they're more murderous
Than wolves, with no inborn restraint,
No code for peace which might allow
Retreat or dignified surrender.
Strange choice of symbol used for love
And tenderness, and yet, because
They're beautiful, they serve.

TWO BLUE DRESSES

What I should wear outweighs
Almost every speculation,
As if clothes could disguise.
A method to evade other
Uncertainties, and yet
The details of a costume
Recollected serve to fix
The character of past events.

The era of that blue silk dress
Totally different from
The year I fell in love, revived
My aunt's old cashmere blue.
Its bias cut and open-work,
That silver buckle-clasp
Low on the hip, enchanted me,
Though out of fashion then.
The very fact became supporting.
I felt a heroine –
And just as well, those first weeks
Of my first, unfortunate,
Short-lived affair. The stylish frock,
Eleventh-birthday gift,
All ruched, had skirt and sleeves puffed out.

I can remember how
I stood and posed before the glass
Entranced, and half afraid
To see reflected in my eyes
The probability
Of loneliness, but more, the wish
For all that came to pass.
I recognized the destiny

I still attempt to grasp.
I nerved myself to welcome it.

That moment, proud in finery,
Has seared my memory
More deeply than the tears I shed
In cashmere, in despair –
The end and the commencement
Of my girlhood, two
Shop-window mannequins
Who almost seem alive.

GOD'S LANGUAGE

Angels have no memory,
God's language no grammar.
He speaks continually,
All words variations
Of his name, the world a web
Of names, each consonant
Proclaims a further meaning;
The unacceptable
Also the true, beyond
Time's bondage. Thus angels
Forget all contradictions,
Accepting every statement
As a commentary.
Their purpose is to gaze
Upon God's works, and listen,
Until the day that he
Pronounce the name: Messiah.

VELASQUEZ'S 'CHRIST IN THE HOUSE OF MARTHA AND MARY'

You stare out of the picture, not at me.
Your sad, resentful gaze is fixed on what
Is only seen reflected in the mirror
On the wall behind your shoulder, perspective
Through an archway cut from sandy slabs of stone
The same warm brown from which you wove your bodice.
That old servant by your side is whispering
Admonitions and consolation – her
Country wisdom. But your attention lapses
From those words of resignation as much
As from the pestle lax within your hand,
The plate of fish, white eggs and pewter spoon,
Wrinkled chilli and broken garlic cloves
Strewn across the table: this, your world,
Precise, material – all you yearn to leave,
Though fear and duty hold you. You cannot find
Courage for the negligence of faith
To justify a gesture similar,
And so what right to join your sister there?

MY GRANDPARENTS

Museums serve as my grandparents' house.
They are my heritage – but Europe's spoils,
Curios from furthest isles,
Barely compensate the fact
That all were dead before I was alive.

Through these high, dust-free halls, where
Temperature, humidity, access,
Are regulated, I walk at ease.
It is my family's house, and I
Safe and protected as a favoured child.

Variety does not exhaust me.
Each object witness to its own
Survival. The work endures beyond
Its history. Such proof supports me.
I do not tire of family treasures.

Because no one remembers who they were,
Obscure existences of which I am
The final product, I merit
Exhibition here, the museum's prize,
Memorial to their legend.

THE CLIMBER

That light before the dawn,
Almost the light of negatives,
All grey, when everything
Shows clear and isolate,
So frail, so separate each twig
Each stone upon his path,
So lonely without colour yet.

The wind is strongest then,
Howls down the mountain side,
Is bitter cold. After the night,
The deepest tiredness assails
That climber who had thought
To reach the heights before
This moment of life's ebb.

Perhaps new day will never come.
Such light prefigures something else,
Another night behind
The distant peaks, or some
Further ordeal, demand,
Upon what strength he cannot feel
But hopes to find.

DISGUISE

She took the brush, began
To paint herself all black.
The bristles dragged in streaks
Between the hairs along her arms.

She paddled paint
Over her breasts.
How that would frighten him
When he undid her dress.

Her cheeks were soon blacked out
One stroke across the brow
Another down her nose
The powder caked her lips
Thickened beneath her chin.
Its taste was bitter.

But she was painted out,
A ghost, a negative,
Released by this disguise
From everything (yes:
Life, Death, Love,
Him: everything).

THE BETROTHAL

What is this, why do they wrestle in the grass,
Tear the clothes that separate their skins?
If she wishes to defend herself, why
Do her limbs melt, why does she strain closer?
Even the earth is more caressing than he.
Crumbling, it blots her cool from his sweat,
Its dryness soothes the chafe of their grinding.
And the rosebay-silk, whiteness unfurling
From split pods, confirms that love is precious.

And he, what is he doing? He's forgotten
Who she is. Something is pulling him down
To the earth's centre, there's an opening;
The grasses seem to be lashing his back,
Forcing him to push deeper and deeper.
Hair in his mouth and a voice distract.
The strength of this impulse to murder becomes
The fervent, whispered phrase, 'I love you'.

Somewhere else love must be real, but not here.
This is beyond them both. They search each other's
Eyes, but only find themselves, minute,
Plunging through expanded pupils to nothing.
Each iris complicated as a stellar map,
Embarked into that flecked immensity,
Empty silence echoes from the void
In answer to the question, 'Do you love me?'

The field is so deep, its soil a talc of bones.
He's far from her, out between the planets,
But his embrace makes her one with the earth.
She seeks comfort from the dead who support her.
If she could hear them talk, they might explain

What love is – or perhaps the shadow of grass
And rosebay on his back, like hieroglyphs,
Could be deciphered, if she exchange
The rest of her life as payment for the answer.

ISOLATES

Apart from present slights
And the more distant, larger,
Still effective hurts,

They brood about the bomb,
The planet's imminent destruction,
All human insignificance;

Those city isolates
In parks, on benches,
Absorbed beyond awareness

Of the rain, and how it plasters
Thinning strands of hair
Against their vengeful temples.

THE FIELD

The field is trampled over utterly.
No hidden corner remains unchurned.
Unusable henceforth for pasture:
Sheep and cattle must feed elsewhere.

The field was torn by battle, dull
Explosions, trenches dug for shelter,
Vehicles which wheeled, reversed,
Hunted down the last resistance.

The field is strewn with bones and metal.
Earth which had not felt the air
During millennia, is now revealed
To every element and influence.

The undersoil surprises by its richness.
In battle's lull, at night, the farmer crawls
To estimate what might be salvaged
Of his lone field's potentiality.

If he survives, the field holds promise
Of great abundance, a yield astonishing,
Unprecedented as all he hopes for.
The field is fertile. He must survive.

NEIGHBOR

Too much happens to some people,
Leaves them no time to deepen.

They are completely different
From the well-adjusted citizen.

Oh, the houses, the journeys,
That have taken my energies.

But then I was younger
And believed myself stronger.

Now I seem to exist
In a torrent of wind

Incurably foreign
As an insect or Martian,

Cannot understand the purpose
Or note more than the surface

Of my neighbor's true quality —
He remains a mystery.

So little happens to some people
And yet they know a secret

Which sustains them, which I cannot
Learn, or long ago forgot.

A FAIRY STORY

The princess in the fairy story
Discovered that a happy ending
Had unexpected consequences.
The castle in the wood concealed
A certain chamber. Her knight revealed
A taste for flagellation. And when
He tired of protests and capitulation,
He rode away – until another kingdom,
Dragon, maiden who could not be won
By any simpler method, was stumbled on.

He then would stay, enter the lists.
He loved the risk, the praise, that combat
Or the guessing game where death
Remained the final forfeit. He loved
A distraught princess, never could resist.
Their fear attracted, their wavering spirit.

Once upon a time, their taming was
The reason for his quest, but now exhaustion,
Boredom, made him pleased his dragon-
Surrogate could test them first.
If they survived the monster's ardent breath
That smoky taint made them delicious.

The rescued princesses compared
Sad stories, boasted of their sufferings,
Exaggerating the ordeal.
They dressed each others' hair, changed
Robes and jewels, waited impatiently
To see the girl who next would join them.

One day, outside the crumbling walls
Of some obscure and unimportant
Principality, the knight was bested.
The dragon fled, dragging bruised coils
Through hedges, across muddy plough-land.
The princess would not follow him,
But turned her back and went inside the town.
The watchers were not more nonplussed.

The knight rode home, sent messages
To all his friends. They drank and sang,
Tortured his wives – they had a ball.
Next day he bade farewell to each
Blood-brother, each noble companion,
Vowed the remaining years to penance
Somewhere far from this vile shambles.

But first, before he set off with his squire
Down that faint narrow path which lured
Deep into the misty forest,
A splendid tomb must be constructed:
Memorial to those princesses,
Obedient victims of his destiny.
The monument still stands, although
The castle fell to ruins long ago.
The knight died on a battlefield.
Their legend: fatalistic, gory,
Fit matter for a fairy story.

GRACE-NOTES

My solemn simplicities, my vows,
My protestations. Tum-te-tum.
Self-accusations. I don't know how
To free myself, to overcome.
Except sometimes, a bird or a tree,
The light on the marsh – direct,
Without equivocation – speak
Of a power that seeks no effect
Outside itself, existing purely,
For which there are no synonyms.
It's a zone I approach unsurely,
That harsh place – where no hymning
Can drown the weak, explaining voice,
Nor grace-notes disguise the wrong choice.

from

Another Full Moon, 1976

VERTICAL

Who told me my place?
It takes generations
To breed such a true believer,
Centuries to produce
Someone who instinctively knew
The only movement possible
Was up or down. No space
For me on the earth's surface:
Horizontal equates with delusive
When only the vertical
Remains open to my use. But
I am released by language,
I escape through speech:
Which has no dimensions,
Demands no local habitation
Or allegiance, which sets me free
From whomsoever's definition:
Jew. Woman. Poet.

THE LACE-WING

Does the lace-wing see me? I stare
Into its pin-point ruby eyes, head on,
At its bristly mouth-parts, my nose
Brushing antennae; the frail body
And intricate veined wings an often-cited,
Not quite clinching, proof of God's existence.

When I look away the lace-wing turns
Abruptly, as if dismissed or freed.
Its shoulder-pivot swings a thread-leg forward.
It moves briskly across my paper,
Then disappears under a corner.

The intensity of our mutual
Examination exhausted me.
We almost exchanged identities.
Our pupils throbbed with the same shared
Awe, acknowledgement and curiosity.
We met beyond confine of size or species.

Next day, the lace-wing still is here.
It clings to the window-frame, drinking
Sunlight. It survives for its moment.
And what sustains our two existences
Remains as much a mystery as God.

DINNER-TABLE CONVERSATION

for Robert Lowell

I began to describe that female connivance
With the man who is duping you: amusement
Overruling outrage and even self-protection;
Like recognising an art-form, appreciating
A fine performance, evaluating this
Particular one's potential for damage:
Ignoring entirely that it's you who will be
The material worked on, you who'll get hurt.

Women who feel such things, the man at my right side
Told me (he had questioned me closely, to make sure
I meant what I was saying), women who know
These truths must relent, then assume and accept
The role of Muse with its hampering duties.
I sensed more than a touch of malice
In his assurance. It was judgement and dismissal:
No trace of kindness there, no praise or glory.

What I was trying to explain, though not
Succeeding (he surely had his reasons
For refusing to listen) was how awareness
Of this split is exactly the fault-line on which
I must build my own San Francisco: the place
Where hazard reigns and poetry begins.
Would I be less a woman or more a poet
Denying my own triumphs and defeats?

He would never surrender his right to be hurt:
He needed a Muse to hate. How glad I was
My calmness could disconcert. He would not

Even grant we shared a common dream. I filled
My glass. We shall soon be forced into the mud,
Consumed by the same worm. Until then (I confess)
I can still be as easily pleased by a man
As by the moon, a tree, a child, or my dessert.

THE BOAT

Who is that person I see   distant   so busy
on the opposite shore   I should join her
she's waiting
a winter tree with scratching twigs
that won't let the wind be its master
she looks like me
but I'm drifting away   slipping   a boat
from its mooring   out   to the centre of the lake
where I'll float and sleep and dream
a black boat
in the heavy colourless silence   empty
simple   with no purpose   while light
withdraws below the water's surface
and the mountains concentrate themselves
fold into their centres
numbed with cold   lulled by monotony
as the black boat plunges through the one
sliver of red left   blood in mercury
from the already set sun
last trace of memory
to be eased away by water
before vanishing

LAST DAYS

i.m. B.S.J.

The confirmed suicide, calm and relaxed,
Reassures sometime-anxious friends.

They hope he's recovered, and he breathes deep
Like one escaped from the evil wood, from the need
To fight off every comer.

There the festooning snakes, fierce creatures
He wrestled with between clustering roots
And choking vines, now are flaccid
As cloth toys, punctured balloons, deflated tyres.
But Laocoön and his two sons together
Were never so assailed.

Like a firm machete cut, that gasping, joyous thrust
Through to the meadow of death.

He's there already. No need to hurry.
The decision made, he can linger a while
On the grass, in the sunshine. Nothing will hurt him.

Only that bruised fist of cloud, still
Almost hidden below the horizon,
That abrupt-rising flock of cawing birds,
The rusty lichen marking the eastern direction
Flaring suddenly into their vision
So the hedges seem wounded,
And one hot gust of wind, indicate
The lull before the storm's destruction.

AUGUST FULL MOON

Whichever I choose to look out from, here in my study,
Where the desk is placed in a corner between two windows,
I see her, the August full moon. Labouring towards
This completion, since yesterday she has freed herself,
Purged and dissolved the humours distorting her shape,
Making her swollen and clumsy, darkened from yellow
Of faded leather into the streaked, mottled red of an
Old woman's cheek. As if she had discharged her poisons
Into my veins, today I was almost demented,
Sodden, confused, barely awake or able to move
About the house and garden. But the moon, silver
In a starless sky, windless night after a day
Of stasis and sunshine, is disdainful of such effects
On whoever is weak enough to suffer this draining
Connection to her necessities: I, who sit yawning and
Trembling in spite of the heat of a perfect evening,
Who will soon go, defeated, to bed, to escape beyond
Dreams into emptiness from this moment when
The universe combines against me, to wait until all
The spheres lurch forward one notch and leave space again
For an opening that hope and change might stream through.

ANOTHER FULL MOON

Another full moon. I knew without checking
The date or the almanac. Again I am
Tearful, uncertain, subdued and oppressed.
It becomes more an abasement each time
To acknowledge I still respond,
Anachronistic as an astrolabe,
Reliable as litmus paper.
No hope of escape, though I should much
Prefer not to be absolutely in thrall
To the rhythms of ocean and cosmos, such
A solemn primitive, a mantic pauper.
With her roughened tongue, the moon curdles
My milk of human kindness. Her maniac
Yellow eye glares through the curtain
And follows every movement. Her purpose
Is obscure, random and cruel.
It is worse than being a prisoner, because
Between her appearances, I forget how she
Rules me, how her gauntleted hand crushes
The back of my neck, forcing me lower,
Making me grovel, ridiculous and
Awful as a manticore. I wonder
If only this is possible, if it must be
True that there will never be space
For wit or humour in the universe
We share, and for all my days I shall bear
The scars of her torture, marked forever
As her creature and her fool.

THE OTHER

Whatever I find if I search will be wrong.
I must wait: sternest trial of all, to sit
Passive, receptive, and patient, empty
Of every demand and desire, until
That other, that being I never would have found
Though I spent my whole life in the quest, will step
From the shadows, approach like a wild, awkward child.

And this will be the longest task: to attend,
To open myself. To still my energy
Is harder than to use it in any cause.
Yet surely she will only be revealed
By pushing against the grain of my nature
That always yearns for choice. I feel it painful
And strong as a birth in which there is no pause.

I must hold myself back from every lure of action
To let her come closer, a wary smile on her face,
One arm lifted — to greet me or ward off attack
(I cannot decipher that uncertain gesture).
I must even control the pace of my breath
Until she has drawn her circle near enough
To capture the note of her faint reedy voice.

And then as in dreams, when a language unspoken
Since times before childhood is recalled
(When I was as timid as she, my forgotten sister —
Her presence my completion and reward),
I begin to understand, in fragments, the message
She waited so long to deliver. Loving her I shall learn
My own secret at last from the words of her song.

THE DEMONSTRATION

Of course I'd throw my children from the sleigh:
Last, frantic bid to gain time. If only
The wolves hold off a while longer.
If only the horses are strong enough.
We race across the steppe,
Horizon dark as a Palekh box
And the wolves' mouths red as inside the box.
When will their hunger be sated?
Are there enough children? Better, perhaps,
Not to survive such exposure of lust
To remain alive at any cost.

Nothing too precious or sacred to sacrifice.
I'll tell you all my secrets in desperation –
Secrets I drag into the gaudy light and betray
To evade the question to guard my privacy
(Such is the style of my conversation)
If only you'll leave me alone.

I'll slip from my coat, leave my skin between your hands
Like a moulting snake. I'll breed another family
And feed the wolves again, veer and dart
Back past the ermine spoor across the snow
To match your questions against my frankness,
To the place where you are waiting:

Where my bones will be broken and hammered and ground
And carbonized, and that black powder strewn
Over the bloody residue.
And then we'll rise, re-made, re-vivified,
Intact – my children and I – and the wolves
At the runners, whose hot breath fouls the sleigh
Where my children and I prepare another demonstration.

HAIR

We with the curly hair belong
To ocean, those whose tresses lie
Close to the skull, fall straight, are claimed
By all sweet waters, brooks and rivers.
Thus for our crown.

                          But body's growth
Affirms the spiral: torso and
Limbs attired in robe of such fine-
Woven mesh of undulation,
Whether conch-coiled or sparse as down.

The salty powers control. Dew-pools
And clouds submit at last to tides.
The moon throws shadows on your face
But glints triumphant on the three
Places that always taste of sea:
Looking into whose waves we drown.

THE FALL

Once you start falling, you fall forever.
Once you let go, there's no hold anywhere.
Wherever your home was, having left it
There can be no other. As a meteor,
Brightness increasing with velocity,
Hurtling through space, need never intersect
Any planet's orbit, you will not find
A resting place — nor end your journeying
Until you've used up everything, consumed
Whatever feeds itself to you, is drawn
Into the plunging vortex of your fall:
Dark path you hope will lead furthest of all.

BURNT PAPER

Papery eyelids, like curves of burnt paper
Which crumble the moment they're touched but
Until then, hold their form. Your eyelids
Are exactly the colour of burnt paper:
Gunmetal grey, dangerous shade, metallic
Glints in the creases around your eyes.

Eyelids like moth-wings, the same dusty,
Downy texture as a moth I saw once, with
A crest of hair fine as a sable paintbrush
And wings that seemed to be sheathed by scales,
A mosaic spangled with plaques of light:
Your eyelids, moving rapid as moth wings or
Fragments of torn paper – love letters
Whirling in the updraft of a fire.

OTHER ROOMS

Afternoon, lying down, my eyes shut.
Winter afternoon, but the birds seem loud.
There's an air of spring, the days are lengthening.
I never remember, with my eyes closed,
Which room, or where it is. So many rooms.
So many sleepless nights, tired afternoons.
This feeling of weakness, of bleeding to death
Without pain or effort, while deep in the wet cold earth
Roots stretch and start to come to life again.
I know I shall get up when the lights come on and
Evening arrives. By then, I'll be certain where I am,
Wide awake, in control, with no thought for
The timid buds determined to survive
Through next month's frost, no lingering doubts
Nor memory of any other room.

WAKING

Sometimes one wakes, leaving the night world behind
As casually as though it could be approached
At any time, as unconcerned as if it need
Never be entered again. Dreams slide away
Like sea-water streams from the limbs of a swimmer
Coming up the beach, knees lifted high,
Clambering over invisible hurdles.

Almost black, the strands of weed that cling
To his arm, the sand-grains blocked by chevrons of hair
Down shin and thigh. The element has marked him
Intimately, everywhere. But he shakes it off,
Wipes salt from his eyes, like a sleeper surfacing,
And does not remember the dangers – the slow sea worm,
Skin soft and rough as tripe, the wrecks and angel-fish,
The mermaids with their coral knives –
That splendour and turbulence to which, as sure
As tides flow back, he must return each night.

APPEARANCE

Profiled, legs striding, arms held clear
Of his sides, mouth and eyes arched,
Pharaonic, head glistening
From sunlight or annointing –
A brief moment only I see him,
Superimposed against the trees and sky
At an angle which proves
His dimension is other than mine.

Here the day is cloudy, but his limbs
Gleamed, rounded by a stronger light.
Moving urgently, vanishing,
(For him the path continued),
What pavement did he tread, that messenger?
Between whom was he travelling?
He will explain everything, later,
Reveal the purpose of appearances.
I wait our next appointment. I trust
In his return. I shall be grateful.

GLASS-THOUGHTS

Honesty, clarity, simplicity.
No hiding behind equivocations —
No dancing veils, false modesty.
Speak out in your own name.
The more revealed, the less unique
You'll see your anguish is,
The more you'll speak for everyone.

I prate of freedom, but what am I
That cannot be contained in the word, 'fear'?

What I have done (and left undone) through cowardice.
Recollect and contemplate. Without judgement.
This is what happened: clear neutral facts,
As clear as glass, and glass contracts, cracks mar
Windows which were never hit or jarred —
Thus self-esteem diminishes.

Glass, slow liquid, rigid and upright,
But unreliable as the citizen
Personifying those virtues:
Myself, behind the glass
Reflecting shoddy dreams of triumph.
No matter how close I stand to another,
Glass separates, a formal boundary.
Are you encased as I am?
Do you yearn to break the glass but lack the courage,
Recoil if asked to damage
Even the wrought bars of your glass prison?
Are they your tears, vitrified?
Have you exuded
This curdled crystal
As scorn and envy?

Encased, immovable, no action possible,
You're forced to watch the past upon that screen:
Opaque now, though once it wavered like water
And seemed to restrain nothing
From flowing outwards or towards you.

Some influence from the past,
Generations of submission
Shocked by repeated uprooting, defeats me.
I construct these traps, dig my own pitfalls,
Arrange scenarios of humiliation.
A net of rusted metal descends and suffocates.
In the battle I lose every advantage.
One after the other my assets fail.

The glass is silvered by vanity,
Traps me in endless duplications of falseness.
Those actions are dimensionless, ghosts
Warped by reflection, flattened by glass.

I will be neither judge nor warrior.
That is not me in the mirror.
It is a false exposure.
It has no depth.

The glass congeals into a crystal egg,
Gathers the waters:
Oil-fouled puddles, ocean's density, my tears.
I hold the egg to my eye.
It reverses everything.
Magnifies
Distorts
Enchants
Protects
                    All my failures and attempts.

POMPEIAN DREAMS

That lamp of pale brass,
Roughly shaped and finished,
Wick twisted from goats' wool
Pulled off the fence
Where it clung to the wire,
Filled with the olives' last pressing
Too rancid for anything else,
Its cone of smoky flame
Sullenly burning. Even
Through sleep, the vapours
Trouble our nostrils.

We're resting on couches
In the stiff, ungainly postures
Of corpses caught by the lava.
And outside the house,
Which stands near the edge of the cliffs,
Dim moonlight and vague
Shudders of summer lightning,
Hiss of the hidden sea,
Seem part of the dream:
A noontime darkened
By ashy eruption.

The whine of a Vespa,
The moan as its motor shifts gear,
Echoes through glinting
Labyrinths of the ocean's
Inner ear: another
Sound-effect to add
To the rush and stamping of bulls,
The droning of insects,

And those muffled prayers and screams
That force their way into
Our dull Pompeian dreams.

BERGAMO COLLAGE

Space packed with vanishing points:
angels and crucifixes
angles and perpendiculars,
as if this place includes more than
the three dimensions,
as if the eras pressed
contemporaneous and coexistent.
Another arch
another curve
another flight of stone
launched from the Celtic base, the citadel
beseiged by Barbarossa.
Pale towers soar,
air
narrowing
between,
compressed impossibly,
then surging out, released from time and piety,
from pride of weathering Venetian lions.

The pillars strain.
Roofs mount the sky.
The dome is buttressed down into earth's centre.
A green-winged angel lifts its arm
to indicate eternity —
wing and arm raised in the same perfect gesture —
or else, perhaps, that Christ
whose painted wounds congeal and fade
as his disjointed wooden body slackens,
darkens, seems more like the tortured Everyman
of sorrows those black-sprayed slogans
on the wall outside evoke —
more apposite for this particular moment —
God's potent new names for men of faith
who will no longer be led
by what made all this live
(and still can hold each building upright).

MY POSITION IN THE HISTORY OF THE
TWENTIETH CENTURY

Strange, how I've never lacked a certain confidence,
Been so dissatisfied with face and body
That I couldn't cheer myself by posing at a mirror,
Sucking cheeks in, raising eyebrows disdainfully.
Small, trim, not especially sturdy or slender,
Large-chested (though small breasted), rather,
It's been a comfort to study the disparities between
Fineness and toughness, my own special markings.
I am not troubled that most people are taller.
Eyes always meet on the same level.

Lucky to live where it was not dangerous
To look like me (no need for a yellow star).
My good fortune took me far from the Holocaust
– Though it's easy to imagine how it feels
To read those scrawls on the station's tiled wall,
To be the African from whose shocked, sick face
I had to turn away when I sensed how he hated me
Watching his pain, knowing we both knew
He could not pretend those words did not stigmatise.
His appearance as much his expression and pride
As mine is – but I can still believe that white skin
Is not yet a primary signal to trigger hostility.

Because what I'm describing is privilege:
The being – soma and psyche – of one who expects
And depends on such luxuries as acknowledgement,
My self-image never subjected to a real test:
Who has not felt anonymous, numbered, docketed,
Trapped and reduced into hopelessness by gross,
Inexpressive matter until the only desire left

Was for a magic formula to make me vanish.
I flaunt my being manifest
To whoever wishes to read the signs,
And what seemed most private and unique in me
I find dependent on my place and time.

(London, 1972)

DRUNK MOON

New moon plunges into a deep well,
Topples over the parapet and vanishes.
A night so dark not even the moon could see
Where he was going. A drunk stumbling into
A flooded ditch, the moon lets go of the edge and
Plummets down the brick-lined sides: a steel ball
Shot through a pipe, a meteor racing away
From the telescope. The moon waning. The shock
Of his fall, the water's icy cold, will sober him up.
He'll have to climb out, find mossy hand-holds.
That's his face you see: clearer, larger, mounting –
The waxing moon, lurching toward the always
Perfect circle of the well's opening. (Only
His clumsy movements make it seem to change shape,
Till his re-emergence blurs the rim completely.)
Full moon: those few short days of music, horseplay
And love for the toper until his next fall.

MOON

Moon, like a bruised rose-petal
Sinking into a small pool, like
A disk of metal, pendant
Of a Saxon necklace, fragile,
Almost corroded through
By time and soil's acids,
Earth's ceaseless tiny shifts
And movements. Moon, I look at you
And think of Japanese prints,
Of mist and sad, cloistered ladies.
Moon, floating over the marshes
Like a fine slice of Prague ham,
Tender, pink, nearly translucent –
Oh, angelic gluttony!
Old reliable Moon, who
Always makes me write poetry.
My sister Moon.

THE PHOENIX

Until you put it to the test,
Into the fire,
You never know
If your fair bird is phoenix true —
If you had skill
to recognise the signs.
You'll wait, and hope. The flames
Too fierce to see or guess
What transformation will result:
Whether the cooling crucible
You lit will show
Only dead ash —
Too late then for regret
When what you loved you killed —
Or if the miracle
Should come to pass: the phoenix rise
Transmuted, purified, unhurt,
Strengthened, renewed,
And grateful for
Your cruelty and trust.

from

***Sibyls and Others*, 1980**

A SIBYL

Her eyes have an indrawn look,
like a bird hatching its eggs.
To whose voice is she listening?
Anxious, the questioners, waiting
those words, but she seems relaxed
and calm, turning the leaves
of her book, does not even
glance down before her finger
points the message: this cave
familiar as a nest,
and she, its rightful tenant —
no longer forced to make
a choice between two worlds.

AENEAS' MEETING WITH THE SIBYL

Hunched over rustling leaves spread out
before her on the stony ground, like a skinny
gypsy with a joint dripping ash in the corner of her mouth
quizzing the Tarot cards, pulling the shabby
shawl closer round elbows and shoulders, then squinting
shrewdly sideways up at a nervous client,
the Sibyl greeted Aeneas. 'Don't tell it from them,'
he pleaded. She was sitting cross-legged, right at the door
of her cave, and he'd heard how often the wind (Apollo!
he thought, it's draughty here, no wonder she looks
so pinched and cold) shuffled the leaves into total
confusion, which she didn't seem to notice or
amend. 'Don't show them to me. Say it in words.'

'You're all the same,' she grumbled. 'Always wanting
more than you pay for. Of course' – tilting her head
sideways on that mole-strewn stringy neck
(he saw white hairs among the dusty curls)
an inappropriate cajoling smile
distorting her archaic features – 'if you give me
something extra,' she wheedled, 'I'll do you a special.'
The tattered russet-purple layers of skin
and cloth wrapped around her body dispersed
an ancient odour of sweat or incense as her movements
stirred them. Through a hole in the skirt he glimpsed a lean
and sinewy thigh, and feet bound up in rags.
'Come inside, young man,' she ordered. 'We'll be private
                                                  there.'

Remembering what came next: his search for the golden
bough, their descent into Hades, the twittering shades,
his painful meeting with Dido, the Sibyl's answer
to Palinurus, and then, at last, embracing
Anchises his father, and learning the destiny
of their descendants, the future of Rome,
Aeneas found it hard to reconcile
his first impressions with the awesome figure
who led him safely through the realm of death
and to the daylight world again. He looked
back from the shore to where she crouched outside
her cave, waiting for another questioner,
and saw she had assumed the same disguise.

THE CUMAEAN SIBYL I

She was the one who, three by three,
burned her books of prophecy
when the asking price would not be met.
Like a wise old nurse who knows that children
rage and fret, but when night comes
creep back into her arms, she watched
the flames, abstracted, stern, and calm.

Her face seemed veiled, the net of lines
a mask, a zone of darker air,
penumbra of another atmosphere –
as though she stood before a fire
deep in her cave, brooding upon
time past and still to come, far from
this splendour and destruction.

Tarquinius Superbus gasped
and broke the silence. 'I'll pay your price.
More than my purse or mother, Sibyl,
is your worth to me, your prophecies
and wisdom.' 'The same price as for all
the nine.' 'Agreed.' She raised her hand,
the fire died, the last three books were saved.

THE CUMAEAN SIBYL II

Because she forgot to ask for youth
when Apollo gave her as many years
as grains of dust in her hand, this sibyl
personifies old age: and yet
those withered breasts can still let down
celestial milk to one who craves
redemption: a dry tree, not a green,
the emblem of salvation.

FROM THE SIBYLLINE BOOKS

(book V. verses 512–530)

Threatening every star, I saw the sun's gleaming sword-blade,
the moon's rage between lightning flashes. The stars were at
war:
God allowed the fight. For instead of the sun, flames
thrust from the east like searching beams of light, and stopped
the two-faced revolution of the moon's changes.

Lucifer fought hard, mounted on Leo's back.
Wily Capricorn attacked young Taurus: with murderous
razor horns, bull and goat bled out their future.
Draco surrendered the Buckle and Belt. Gemini
and Virgo invaded Mars. The bright Pleiades vanished.
Pisces overthrew the realm of Leo: in dread of whom,
Scorpio destroyed himself with his poisoned tail.
Orion smashed the Scales, and armoured Cancer fled,
scuttling away from the whirling club of that mighty hunter.
Sirius, dog-star, succumbed, vanquished by the sun's heat:
Aquarius consumed by ardent Lucifer.

Heaven itself was stirred at last to fiery wrath.
Horizon to zenith, the firmament shook, stunning the warriors,
plunging them headlong down into Ocean's waters.
The hissing trail of their fall kindled the whole earth.
The sky remained starless, all constellations darkened.

A DESERT SIBYL

A ranting middle-aged albino,
open-mouthed, eyes blurring, sightless:
that gaunt sharp-featured desert sibyl

who journeyed through the parching dunes
and past the heights of Mount Tibesti
up from Lake Chad with her sacred ibis

intent that all should hear her message,
verses Tanit's power inspired:
warning for Dido, queen of Carthage.

THE HEBREW SIBYL

I who was driven mad and cast out
from the high walls of Syrian Babylon
I who announced the fire of God's anger
who prophesy to those about to die
divine riddles
am still God's oracle.

Mortals in Hellas will claim me
name me as from another city of birth —
Erythrae — one of the shameless.
Others will say I had an unknown father
and my mother was Circe
brand me a crazy impostor.

But when all has taken place
when the walls collapse and the Tower crumbles —
that coming time, when knowledge is lost
and men no longer understand each other —
no one will call me insane
but God's great sibyl.

SIBYL OF THE WATERS

Noah's daughter
sibyl of the waters

first sibyl
the most ancient

with Shem, Ham, and Japhet
saw her father naked

already she had prophesied
the flood

and understood
it was the nakedness of God.

Arms raised in invocation
officiating at the altar

where the Ark had grated
upon Ararat

she placed the burning brands
shielding her face

then crushed the dove to death
against her breast:

an ominous
propitiation.

THE DELPHIC SIBYL

The tripod, the laurel leaves, the robe and style
of a virgin, though I was an honest widow of fifty:
because of my sober gaze and my docility,
the elders of Delphi chose me and taught me
what had to be done with the tripod and laurel leaves.
They offered a drink from the holy stream, showed me
the cleft in the rock where I must sit and breathe
mephitic fumes and chew the leaves until
my head began to swim and words came blurred.
Those gentlemen of Delphi's best, most ancient
families, our city's noble priests,
quite overwhelmed me. I was a simple woman,
obedient, eager to please, and honoured
by the role. And even had I wanted to,
been bribed to do, there was no chance
to slant the auguries. Petitioners
would proffer written questions first to them,
and their interpretations of my drugged
and mumbled ravings were determined by
Apollo's demands and the city's political needs.
I was an ideal oracle, they told me.
Thus I grew old, though monthly more confused,
appalled, exhausted, and in every way
the opposite of all I once assumed.

DESTRUCTION OF A SIBYL

Right from the start, the Pythia was depressed.
Every omen came unfavourable.
He'd been on duty at the sanctuary
and afterwards, telling his friend Plutarch
about the catastrophe, Nicander, one
of the priests at Delphi, could still remember her screams.

She'd gone into the proper trance, but how
reluctantly; at once began to speak
in a strange, hoarse voice. Whatever dumb and evil
spirit had possessed her would not reveal
its origin. No curse the priests pronounced
could banish it, protect her or themselves.

Like a ship on a stormy sea, foundering,
when bales of precious cargo are jettisoned
and the galley-slaves pull harder and faster because
of the lash, though their oars have splintered, she lurched
and shuddered, struggling to escape; tried to crawl
on bleeding hands and knees toward the door.

That cowardice could never be purged. No matter
how long they lived, the whole College of Priests
would not forget the shame. Everyone fled.
Contagion of fear: panic alone had ruled.
Apollo's priests abandoned their oracle,
and when they returned, found her broken and changed.

Python uncoiled himself, in all the glistening
length of his body, come back to remind them of

the ancient goddess, the Mother Apollo usurped.
It was She who had spoken and claimed the soul
of the Pythia to serve at Her altar and be
Her oracle forever in the underworld.

HEROPHILE

Whenever she stopped at Delphi, Herophile,
the oldest sibyl, would stand on a special rock
and chant her oracle. Long before Helen
was born, she had foretold the girl would grow up
a trouble-maker, the bane of Europe and Asia.

Through forests and over mountains she wandered, but
two towns wrangled for the honour of her birth:
Marpessus the red (whose thirsty soil swallows
the river Aidoneus) and Erythrae.

Sometimes the sibyl said her mother had been
a nymph, an immortal; at others named herself daughter
or bride to Apollo – Artemis, his sister and twin.

When Herophile died, her tomb was built by a stream
in Apollo's temple grove, and guarded by
a stony herm whose blankness seemed to mock
a life of traveller's alarms, poor food,
the sight of too much human misery,
hope and credulity and ceremony,
bad roads, virginity, and solitude.

THE CIMMERIAN SIBYL

These habits come from the old place,
customs brought from home: almost
the only memories of endless
trees, a northern waste of cold
and dark beyond the Caucasus.

Because it was always so, here
on the shores of the Hellespont I still
must have my drum and lance, the three
mushrooms and sacred feathers, before
I rise to heaven and touch the stars.

Everything I know was taught
by the last sibyl able to
recall those days. Crippled, toothless,
and blind, she told me tales of how
we fled the Scythians, and ravaged Thrace.

I learned the steps of the magic dance
(my body burned in trance, the music's
beat made me gulp gallons of water
to quench such thirst), got by heart
the words that trap the reluctant god.

He slides under my skin as smoothly
as the blade of a knife in the hand of one
who slits the pelt and pours warm blood
from the throat of a perfect sacrifice.
Does god or sibyl then pronounce?

But now we are too near Greece, and priests
interpret my oracles, move
between me and the god, stifle my power,
altering the ritual;
fearful; changing the old ways.

HALLUCINATING SIBYL

As though burning upwards,
her waxy flesh become
candle to the flame of Apollo,
entirely possessed,
sibyl of Thrace,
sister of Pythagoras,
hallucinating sibyl.

Flakes of snow swirl and
drift through the cave mouth.
Gusts of wind
intensify the glow.
The brands throb
like the heart still beating between
the split ribcage of the sacrifice.

Entranced before the fire,
open-mouthed, throat and chest
reflecting light like a breast-plate,
naked shoulders shadowed
and glinting eyes rolled white
to see armies clashing,
phalanxes in the heavens

above the roof of the cave:
her mantic vision penetrates
through rocks, earth, roots
of winter-stripped trees,
the turbulent heavy sky
that shrouds the land
from the Euxine sea to the Hellespont.

Further back, beyond
the circle of light,
its range of noisome, pungent
fumes, stand priests
with the dagger and bowl for the blood
she drinks, the skins to clothe her
after she has prophesied.

Candle to the flame of Apollo,
entirely possessed,
sibyl of Thrace,
sister of Pythagoras,
sibyl hallucinating –
but not yet begun
to use Apollo's words or speak with his voice.

SIBYL ON THE RUN

Vague gaze from tired grey eyes
under the wide brim of her hat,
the fine-grained white skin of her face
mud-splashed, hair tangled, uncurling,

harried by wind and rain, she creeps
through the door of the smoky hut, and quick
as a snake, wary and furtive as
a forest animal, thrusts out
a scratched hand to take one
of the oat-cakes from the hearth, crumbles it
into her mouth, gulping with haste

looks round the silent circle of watchers
(no need to doubt, these were believers)
then reassured, straightens her back,
raises her chin, loosens her ragged cloak,
arrogant and proud; announces
herself: the wisest sibyl on earth.

SICK SIBYL

The ecstasy that drives salmon upstream
to spawn and die, eels across oceans,
seal to their breeding grounds, deer hundreds
of miles north (with the wolves who follow
to pick them off), geese winging south,
insects into fatal nuptial
flight, all united by
the spasm that verifies existence —
the ecstasy I never once
have felt: my ecstasy entirely
different, my ecstasy
a self-consuming sickness, an envy
of my questioners, who are one
with everything that lives and feels —
sustained, embraced, and blinded by
the shimmering haze which only my
sick eyes can pierce to see the truth,
the future, and the end of love.

BLOCKED SIBYL

Sullen or stubborn, self-willed,
stupid, or just plain finished
as a sibyl – sometimes it happens
that way: one day, someone
who'd seemed absolutely right
for the job will dry up.
Hair messed, skin blotched, eyes
angrily or hopelessly
averted (but it's easy to tell
she's been crying) she won't answer
even the simple question:
What is it? from her apprentice-attendants,
much less pronounce. Maybe
she's sickened by laurel leaves, smoke
from the brazier, the sweet, foul stench
of anxiety. Better
be blind than always forced
to see those supplicating gestures.
Secretly, they've begun
to appal her – she's afraid that quite
soon she might break down,
weep or laugh with despair
at the most solemn moment. Finished
or freed: she knows as well
as they that she's useless now,
a blocked sibyl.

RESCUE OF THE SIBYL

for Françoise Claustre

After our climb to that distant mountain plateau,
when at last we stood close to the chasm's dangerous edge,
and leaned across the shaky wooden railing
to fathom what lay hidden in its depths,
from that opening rose a smell as harsh as ashes
dowsed with water, a curling vapour dank
and raw as floats above a marshy waste.

An aged creature, her guardian, perhaps,
uncocked his rifle, began his tired patter.
'Those steps lead down to the quaking rocks. In the deepest
cave, our famous sibyl sits on her tripod,
chewing laurel leaves and prophesying.
I am the only one who can interpret
every word she speaks. For a fiver I'll take the lot.'

But we gave him money to go away instead,
and the other two unpacked their sensible macs
and brandy flasks for protection against the damp.
How thoughtless and deprived I felt, as well
as freezing cold. I hadn't prepared myself
at all for the expedition, hadn't even
formulated one serious question.

The sides of the cleft were slick and wet, they curved
away like vertigo. As though peering through torn
drifting cloud from a plane when a current of air clears the curdled
atmosphere, I saw something moving, a horrible
dancing, the stones were revolving, atoms of earth
vibrating and boiling. There were groans and flashes of lightning.
Then the fumes blew back, thicker than before.

The bravest of us moved toward the abyss.
With each rung trod, the turbulence retreated.
She drove it below, a sullen, defeated dragon.
The staircase lay exposed as a flimsy construction
and there, on the mud and grit at the bottom, stood smudge-pots
and clumsy machines to delude any watchers, convince
them the rocks had been quaking. Ashamed, we followed her steps.

That poor wretch, terrorized and abused,
stammered and rolled back her eyes when we finally found her.
It was months since she'd seen daylight or breathed fresh air.
Between her teeth were half-chewed leaves, and her mouth
and chin were stained from their juice. Anxious and trembling,
like a hostage newly released from her ordeal,
she could not believe that rescue had come through a dream.

THE SIBYLS IN AMIENS CATHEDRAL

Thin-waisted Gothic sibyls
with pale calm faces
under wimples of clean Flanders linen,
holding your classical
attributes in elegant
fingers: the book,
the palm, the sword, the scroll,
images eaten
away and fading back
into the flaking
painted plaster and stone.

I can just distinguish which
is the Delphic one,
the Libyan, the Cumaean,
though your look and style
are those of later days,
Christian times,
your colours the gold and blue
of chapel banners,
soft madder-pink and red
of hawthorn flowers,
lush Somme-river green.

Your sister, the Tiburtine,
told Augustus
of Christ's coming, and so,
as oracles
of his triumph, on these cathedral

walls you stand
with the Prophets – proud pagan women,
half forgotten:
like the message you brought once,
but long ago,
to troubled northern souls.

THE SIBILA

sung at midnight on Christmas Eve by a young boy dressed in a rich, long robe and carrying a sword, in the Church of San Bartolomé and Nuestra Señora de Bonany, co-patrons of Soller de Mallorca, Islas Baleares.

The Day of Judgement comes
when there will be no Holy Service.
The Universal King of man,
God Eternal, then will judge us,
to everyone deliver justice.

Terrible fires will tear Heaven apart.
Lakes, springs, and rivers all aflame.
Even the fish will scream.

To the good He will say,
Come my blessed children
possess the Kingdom
which has been waiting
since the world was first created.

Humble Virgin, who this night gave birth
to infant Jesus, pray
He guard us from damnation's wrath.

With great severity and sternness
to the wicked He will say,
Go, evil ones, to everlasting torment
to the fire eternal,
to the Inferno and your Prince of Darkness.

THE LIBYAN SIBYL

She casts away her clothes like soul's ascent
from the world of matter, shining arms upraised,

appears about to move with the ease of a dancer:
a hind setting its feet on the highest place.

Blinded by heavenly light, her eyes are closed.
What need of text – her message a psalm of praise?

It has come, the triumph of love above understanding:
Eternal ardour, ecstasy, and grace.

THE PERSIAN SIBYL

The Persian sibyl's powers augment with dusk.
She turns her book and face toward the shadow
and waits for revelation; prefers to guess,
not see, the written words – that gentle ageless
witch – and that you cannot read her expression.
The prophesies come clearer now; though she makes
each phrase a merciful apocalypse.

THE PHRYGIAN SIBYL

Speaking the language the first humans spoke
on that mountain plateau, homeland of Kybele,
Great Mother of the Gods, goddess
of caverns and wild beasts – words
only her eunuch-priests now
can understand – always, at the beginning
of spring, when the frenzy of lamentation
and blood-letting has changed to joy
at His rebirth, the Phrygian sibyl
blesses the whole earth – rivers,
herds of horses, flowering vines
and lovers – making the oldest promise
in the name of the Mother: eternal life.

THE SHINTO SIBYL

White snow settles on the sacred peak,
white clouds drift between the cedar boughs,
white bear and antelope, wild boar, run there.
White boulders mark the ever-trodden path.
White the robes the ancient pilgrims wear.
White the sunrise through the eastern door.

Long white hair hung down the sibyl's back,
white flowers from the branches of her crown.
White light reflected by her flashing glass,
white paper fluttered on the stick she bore.
White stone the pavement where the miko danced,
white drum she beat, and white her moving feet.
White sound I could not understand, her song.
Dead-white, but open-eyed, her face in trance.
White eagle-feathers left upon the shrine.
White bird that cried her message to me: 'Pure'.

Note: Miko – priestess, Sibyl

THE TIBURTINE SIBYL

Albunea, nymph and sibyl of Tibur,
from your temple grove above the river's gorge
always you see the world through the mist
of those plunging falls.
                        The plain below spreads wide
and further west, upstream, like Hera's milk,
white water rises from a primal source.
Entering, at first, in spite of its warmth,
you shudder. Then, the sulphur bites, tormenting
as the centaur's poisoned shirt.
                        With head rolled
backwards, sunken-eyed, you prophesy,
and all the richest senators of Rome,
the emperor himself, accept each word
of warning and advice as though the deified
Hercules spoke —
                        whose voice comes forced
and husky from your throat as his was when
he climbed onto the funeral pyre; whose holy
rites you celebrate with mystery,
wild-olive fires and serpent sacrifice:
his priestess, oracle, and virgin-bride.

THE ORACLE AT DODONA

The oak is full of doves, they nest in clefts
among its naked boughs. This oak
is the oldest tree in the world. Homer wrote of it.
Here, Zeus rules with Dione and prophesies
through the throats of doves, doves they call oracles.
Three Doves: three women cloaked in furs,
whose calloused unwashed feet must never break
connection of their flesh from mother-earth.
Doves' voices speak gods' words. The women
stretch their vowels to sound like doves burbling.

Suddenly, the doves' murmuring
is drowned by the clangour of bronze rousing
the sanctuary – chains of a scourge in the hand
of a bronze statue, which every gust of wind
makes clash against a hollow gong and echo.
Someone has come to have his fate confirmed.

The stylos bit into the soft lead strip as he
wrote the question. The Doves approached. They stamped
their feet on the muddy grass. The doves in the trees,
reverberations of bronze, the women's song
and the oak-wood lots in the black, snake-painted jar,
agreed. "Yes." All would be as he wished.

A YOUNG SIBYL

At first she appears
candid and chaste,
yet when she stands
in front of the altar, opens
her mouth, and the voices start
to speak through her throat
in that plangent blare,
everything is changed.
Does she draw down the power
or does the god ride her?

The sanctuary is dark
but her slender form
grows larger, seems
surrounded by a glare,
a holy nimbus.
The odour of stables
is stronger than incense,
and blurring all her phrases,
the snapping of reins
and champing of horses.

Ageless, sacred mare
who gallops unshod,
one of Apollo's steeds,
over past and future.
Those words have meant war.
Blameless though dangerous,
her gnomic sentences
bring secrets back to light,
unriddle old mysteries
and knot new ones.

INTROSPECTION OF A SIBYL

If only I could be aware of what is happening
in that void, that gap, that murky, fathomless cleft
where space and time must exist
between inspiration and the sound of my own voice:
the truth I never once have heard
a moment earlier than my listeners.

But I am no more conscious of the prophecies
than I can understand the language of birds.
A bird is singing now.
In spite of legend, like everyone else,
I wonder and guess at its message.
My oracles come like birdsong — or how I imagine
they must begin to sing: by instinct,
neither needing nor able to think.

The most terrible phrases burst from my mouth.
My profession is to doom strangers.
Already, as a girl,
playing ball with my friends in the village square
or feeding my tame pigeon, I remember
being more appalled than my parents
by what I'd say: an unforgivable insult
dealt out in all innocence, or a blurted sentence
like a gift to confirm good fortune.

How I admire control, and yearn to achieve it.
I've become almost grateful to those who control me.
Before, I never knew when it would begin.
But the closed, startled expressions
on the faces of those standing round
— as though shutters crashed down —

meant again I'd defined or foretold,
unerringly exposed the poor secret
some old man kept hidden all his life:

with sight as sharp as an eagle
who spots the frightened creature
veering back and forth, exhausted,
across a rocky mountainside,
maddened by the shadow of its wings –
and heavier than every element,
surer than the laws of gravity,
swoops for the kill.

After a few times, you recognize
a universal wariness. It takes longer
to fear yourself, to accept the certainty
of never illuminating that blankness,
that vital hiatus when the demon or angel,
the god, perhaps, takes possession
and you don't exist
yet have the power of a god.

Panic of falling – said to be
the sole inborn fear of a human infant.
Deeper than fear, I've learned, lies the greatest pleasure:
nausea and exhilaration of plummeting free,
the glee of surrender to nullity,
temptation more primal
than any craving for security.

And the price for such knowledge? To have
absolutely no command over your life,
your words – no possibility
of calculated effects or tactics or policy.
But how useful you can be to others; and how lucky

if rather than burning or stoning, they protect you,
feed you, and let the simple folk praise you,
keep you safe as a caged bird,
and call you a sibyl.

ONLY THE MAGPIE

Only the magpie among all its kind
had to be caught for the Ark, and ever since
bear Noah's curse. Yet beyond thought, more
acute than any thought, his rush of pale
and dark against the clouds and shooting twigs
evoke that time before the Fall when just
the wish to fly created wings and skill.

In paradise, fulfilment and desire
were close as white to yolk of an egg. Now,
desire destroyed by its pursuit, the bird of joy
cannot evade the hunter's net. Harsh
chatter of magpies out on the lawn. They pose
sidle and hop, pull worms, lift off, and never
wonder which pinion to use first.

THE ROUTE NAPOLEON

Pollarded trees produce new growth:
this year's twigs and leaves displayed
as evidence. Trees marked by cryptic
streaks of paint, posters, reflector-disks
pressed into their trunks, wounds roughly dressed
with tar. Trees planted to absorb
the fumes of traffic, clothe embankments
and disguise the motorway. Trees
used; trees with the hopeless, doomed
servility of mutilated slaves
or trophy prisoners from some
forgotten war. Trees that can
no longer represent another realm
or further possibility,
but stand there, rooted, by the side
of the road, trapped as much as any
speeding driver or his passenger.

DRIVING NORTHWARD

There are stretches of road I remember,
autumn mist moving across a meadow,
driving northward, going home for the winter.

Such landscape is never spectacular,
a moment between dark trees and a river,
an outside curve, stones marking its contour,

and glowing with sunset, a segment
of the circling, luminous heavens.
Places where the unavoidable future

reveals itself: that panicked creature
darting under the car's chassis
as we swerve around the next corner.

TREES

Trees, our mute companions,
looming through the winter mist
from the side of the road,
lit for a moment in passing
by the car's headlamps:
ash and oak, chestnut and yew;
witnesses, huge mild beings
who suffer the consequence
of sharing our planet and cannot
move away from any evil
we subject them to,
whose silent absolution hides
the scars of our sins, who always
forgive — yet still assume
the attributes of judges, not victims.

DEADHEADING THE ROSES

All day I clip the withered blossoms from the roses,
cut back till where at join of stem and leaf
I sense the chance of one more flower.

I work against maturity and the full cycle,
try to stop the dull hips from ripening
and using that energy

I want to move towards more buds and flowers,
repeat the same glory, achieve what yet
I know to be impossible:

rejuvenated immortelles; far easier than
to accept the pressure of further growth,
the destiny that hardens petals

into firm, streaked knobs of seed disdaining beauty
for the sake of the future: that power
the artless rose-bush manifests.

Because every rose on the trellis witnesses how
nothing can halt the closing of one phase
or shorten the interval between

fruition and death. While I tear my hands on thorns
in a losing fight against autumn, the same
wind parching the roses' leaves

is driving me nearer to my destination. Only
some miracle could force new flowering,
another scented season.

NEW YEAR IN ENGLAND

Red tiles on the village roofs
fusing into a smoky glow
the sun's last fanning rays illuminate.
The marshland and hills.
The further arch of winter blue
above the corded nap of new-ploughed fields.
That floating crimson lake of mist.
The clouds also demand their praise,
those purple banners. Yet something is lacking.

This calm afternoon
of early January, when all the world
still feels as if resting from festival,
needs more lauding, more gratitude,
than the empty road and separate houses,
heraldic television aerials,
the silhouetted tower of the vacant
church, seem able to express.
And I wait hopeful and uncertain
if fit words will come: the glory-song
to satisfy such daunting trust.

THE NEW TREE

Planted a tree the afternoon before
what has become the first evening of autumn
(eucalyptus-spring in Australia),
wind dropped and clouds moved on, mid-August storms
seemingly gone. And now the moon, almost
at full, a thin-worn disk of beaten tawny
metal foil or crumpled papery fallen
eucalyptus leaf, hovers above the hawthorn
and the bramble hedges – unkempt corner
of my northern garden – as I cross the lawn
to touch the newly planted tree, its short
rose-madder stems and glaucous foliage, once more
and wonder if its roots can feel the draw
of the antipodes, the pull from that far shore;
wish it well until tomorrow's dawn.

CHILDHOOD

I see it like an illustration in a magazine:
the low and seemly blocks of middle-class apartment buildings,
with half-grown trees and sprinkled lawns between; colours neither
pale nor garish but chosen from the clear, most popular
and tasteful range: grass-green, sky-blue, an undemanding red, and
pointillistic touches from parked cars, fire-hydrants, freshly varnished
doors and window-frames. The streets do not run straight: the land
is hummocky, its dips and curves are on a human scale.

Here on the hill-crest where I stop to contemplate my whole
domain, I feel as powerful and joyful as the wind
that forms the clouds each moment into different shapes.
I wonder at the lives of such exemplary inhabitants,
confirm again that everything's in order, just as it should be
in Toytown; and only then I nod my head and check the straps
and buckles of my skates, let myself go, and swoop down, down,
past houses, families, up the opposite slope and into Heaven.

A CHILD CRYING

Gasps and sobs through the wall from the next flat:
a child's voice in dirge-like complaint whose words
I cannot make out but whose tone accords too well
with my mood – as though it were I in that stranger's room,
bitter and desolate, choked with grief,
oppressed by a world I cannot understand,
that withdraws and refuses to console me.

A child crying. We who can imagine
that to batter the child to silence would be
kinder than to leave it in such distress
(at least would change our own distress), each time
are forced back to that old anguish – hours shut into
a bedroom, crouched behind a slammed door,
stifling in a wardrobe, throbbing temples
pressed against a bathtub; trapped horror
of the cot, suffocating blankets, the sickly
baby colours of their damp itching.

And when at last it has stopped, and the unknown child
is pacified, we are left exhausted and
ashamed as if after torture, capitulation,
and the final loss.

ALMOST-FULL MOON

First through one window
then moving to the other
she looks at me all evening,
sitting at my desk. But
I'm only one of the creatures
the almost-full moon watches.
There are so many rooms and houses
so many open windows
so much to see, such huge
responsibility.
She supervises moths
moles and lizards, owls
orchards and empty beaches,
and wakeful lonely children
who stare up at the face
of the calm white mother,
till soothed, their heads roll sideways
on the pillow, into shadow
and they fall asleep.

THAT SMILE

Sometimes I find myself looking at children
with that fond soft smile of older women
who've forgotten it all – which made me hate them
when I was yearning for confirmation
of a new maternal status, years ago.

But yesterday, though I should have known better
(or else, why remember?) in a carriage
on the Northern Line with a distracted
mother and her two small boys, I felt
the same expression distort my features.

Sturdy, rosy, laughing, zipped into
anoraks, pressing their noses flat
against the windows, the naughty children
crawled across armrests and gabbled nonsense,
ignoring her restraints and protests.

Truer to their humanity than either
of us, they knew, without having to learn,
that for the short time given, whether
it ended at Edgware or in seventy years,
the only purpose of living is pleasure.

Maybe the smile that used to disconcert
had a different meaning. Those other women
might have been trying to reassure
and divert me, as I now wanted
to catch the mother's furious eye

and make her see her own children
as emanations of wisdom, freedom
and joy. (But even more, as empty
station platforms hurtled past, I wished
that she would turn to me and smile.)

UNSUITABLE

When, instead of scrubbing their jeans, I'm rinsing
my smalls, it's not like doing housework (doesn't feel
right: neither justified nor sanctified)
no one to blame or accuse

When I open a box of matches and see one
is broken or shorter, or has a half-formed head,
that's the one I'll use

The tainted grapes on the bunch, those with a spot
of mould, softening away from the stem, I pick and eat
first, and the squashed tomato, blackening banana,
all the bletted fruit

Whatever is perfect or beautiful or new,
I carefully save for a special occasion: a wardrobe
of unworn, old-fashioned shoes

Waiting for something to happen (augmenting impatience)
I sense how others avoid me, fearing a breakdown,
potential of chaos, shattering, splintering glass
as the genie gets loose

And the smile on my face, that calm of the over-cautious
to hide my resentment and envy, is like make-up
on a birthmark or a wound

Because I will not admit what I think, I have no
opinions; never admit who I am, have lost
my history; cannot admit what I want,
have forgotten how to choose

Until this huge discomfort constitutes
my whole existence: called to act a part
for which I'm completely unsuitable.

IT MUST

Friends, sisters, are you used to your face in the mirror?
Can you accept or even recognize it?
Don't be angry, answer me frankly, excuse
the question's crudity. I can't – no matter
how often I take the little square of glass
from my bag, or furtively glance into shop-windows,
the face reflected back is always a shock.

Those scars and wrinkles, the clumping of pigment
into moles, spots, faulty warty growths
around hairline and neck, the way skin's texture is changed
absolutely, become roughened and scaly,
coarse-grained, every pore visible, as though
the magnification were intensified: horrible.
These days, I prefer firmer flesh in close-up.

Younger, I remember staring, with a mixture
of attraction, repulsion, and pity, at the cheeks of older
women – the sort I chose for friends. Did they
need me as much as I idealized them?
There seemed something splendid and brave about such
                                                    raddled
features, crusted and blurred with the same heavy make-up
I've taken to wearing – warpaint, if, as they say,
the real function of warpaint is to bolster
the uncertain warrrior's spirit, more than
to undermine and terrify his opponent.

Now, I long to ask my friends these very
questions and compare reactions, blurt out
the taboo words. But we're so polite, so lavish
with compliments, tender, protective – cherishing

the common hurt: tenderness of bruised flesh,
darkness under the eyes from held-back tears,
watery blisters on frost-touched fruit already
decaying, marked by death's irregularities.

Friends, tell me the truth. Do you also
sometimes feel a sudden jaunty indifference,
or even better, extraordinary moments
when you positively welcome the new
face that greets you from the mirror like
a mother – not your own mother, but that other
dream-figure of she-you-always-yearned-for.
Your face, if you try, can become hers. It must.

DIVINATION BY HAIR

I

Every few days, looking into the mirror,
I find another dozen hairs turned white.
Though dubious about my purpose, almost
despising myself, I go on pulling them out.
She, the ideal I stubbornly adhere to,
would never search so urgently for their wiry
glint, crane her neck awkwardly
the better to ensure not one escapes
the tweezer — disdain pursuit of such
discoveries. White hairs are curlier
and vigorous, age and death becoming
more assertive the closer they approach.

I know it can be nothing but a losing
battle, paltry and ridiculous.
Sooner or later I'll have to choose whether
to be bald or white. I cannot continue
this depilation with impunity.
They'll never grow back as fast as vanity
can raze them. Like one enthralled (more than
mere scrutiny distorts my face)
hours at a time I stand in front of my mirror,
which long before now should have lost its power
and become a superseded altar, not
the secret place of panic, rage, and grief.

I'd prefer to be brave, let my tresses fade
to mottled grey and white — but even the best
resolutions are hard to keep when every
day's attrition brings a new defeat.
If only it could happen overnight:

one morning I would wake transformed into
that dignified wise matron of my dreams,
matured at last to grace (though I make her sound
like the grandmother on a birthday card –
acquiescent, fatalistic, too bland
by far – not at all what I mean)
storms calmed, reefs passed, safe harbour now in sight.

II

Every day, new hairs faded.
Why don't I just accept it?
Why don't I dye it? What difference
would it make if I left them? Age
would not come sooner, nor my actions
avert dissolution and death.
Who do I think I'm fooling?
– No one except myself.
For who cares really whether
my hair is grey, white, or black?
Others, also, are doing their best
to conceal, refuse, forget.

III

Because death always seemed a mother –
or a grandmother, someone
familiar – now I come near
the time of greying hair, I fear
the mask more than the skull beneath.

IV

Silver hair is the warning sign.
To watch it spread is like catching fire.
I want to smother it, to hide
the mark that shows I'm next in line,
exposed, too near the danger-zone.
I feel death creeping up behind.
Those fading hairs and deepening lines
are the entangling net she throws.

V

Witch from an ancient forest-tale;
goddess; hag; Atropos-Fate;
Kali; crone. Can I placate
you better by carefully hiding the blaze
you sear across my brow, or apeing
your style? Conquering queen, your embrace
is inexorable. Whether I hate
or deny or adore you, you will unmake
me, eternally, then create me again.

VI

days   mirror
   dozen hairs   white
   dubious   purpose
despising
      ideal   stubbornly
                  urgently
                  awkwardly
            not one escapes
                  pursuit
discoveries
   vigorous age and death
      assertive   approach.

                        losing
battle paltry   ridiculous
                        choose
      bald or white
                  impunity
                              vanity
                  enthralled
         scrutiny distorts
                              my mirror
                        lost its power
            a superseded altar
                  panic, rage, and grief

            brave   tresses
   mottled grey and white   best
resolutions
      attrition   defeat
                  overnight
                  transformed
   dignified   dreams
                  grace
      grandmother
         fatalistic
   far
      calmed   passed   harbour   in sight

127

SATELLITE

Light streams into the room:
a presence behind the curtains
pushing against their edges
as palpable
menacing and volatile as mercury.
Suspended in an empty sky,
above the black backdrop of pines,
that scalding glare,
flattening the lawn into a bald formality.
How could I forget the full moon?

Only this afternoon
impossible to stop the tears
forced from my eyes and down my face:
a water-mask
seen through the beaded curtain of a cataract.
Again and again I'm dragged off-course.
For days I could not wake — tonight,
quite lunatic,
I cannot sleep, but want to go outside, into
that light, and shriek at the moon.

I hope it will end soon.
And yet, if I withdraw beyond
her rule, through cowardice, or
she no longer
focuses her power and ceases to disturb,
how foiled and desolate I'll be:
a barren victory, gained
by banishment
from that world of extremity in which I've lived
as satellite to the moon.

DANGER-AREAS

The landscape, hazed, recedes in layers,
pale heifers munching in the meadows,
hills crowned with castles as in fairy tales.

Those little touches so essential
to create the state of tension
that brings the picture into focus.

It must be strange. Deceptive comforts
of familiarity are not
effectual, are not allowed.

Otherwise, why does he seek
the dragon; why is she, so languid
at the window, hoping for catastrophe.

Romance, that necessary irritant,
becomes the only explanation
of sojourn in such danger-areas.

AGAIN

Suppose the prince who once had been a toad
changed back after a certain span of years.
Perhaps it always was intended.
Happily-ever-after only meant
a few decades, and this return to earlier
days inexorably programmed into
the experiment. The kindly fairy's
blessing lost its potency as princess
and her golden hero aged together.

Suppose one morning when he woke he felt
the clammy stricture web his toes and fingers,
his mouth begin to stretch into that
recollected lipless grin; and when
she turned to face him from her pillow, saw
in her contracting pupils the reflection
of cold warts and freckles surfacing
like blisters on his muddy skin.
He dared not speak, but waited, numb with dread.

Suppose that night she'd dreamed about the hour
her ball had rolled and splashed into the pool
and that foul toad had hopped towards her, croaked
his arrogant demand, and forced her will.
Yet afterwards, everything was perfect.
As though the time between had vanished, now
she smiled and clung to him, gazed deep into
unaltered eyes. Who could guess the coming
transformation? Let it all begin again.

ANIMAL TAMER

You would have made a good animal tamer —
I can tell by the way you're taming the wild black cat
that appeared last week at the bottom of the garden.
Every morning she comes a little further.
You go outside with a half-filled saucer of milk
and put it down as if you didn't care,
but each day move it an inch nearer the door.

The black cat's glaring eyes have a baffled look.
There's something about you she cannot understand.
You've activated her curiosity.
But still she crouches watchful under the bushes
until you glance away and fuss with your pipe,
and then she dashes across and gulps and laps,
the hair round her neck bristling with suspicion,
peering up at you several times a minute,
relieved yet puzzled by such indifference,
as though she missed the thrill of flight and escape.

Today, for the very first time, you turned and stared
at those yellow, survivor's eyes, and the cat stared back
a moment before she swerved and ran to safety.
But then she stopped, and doubled round and half
gave in, and soon, as I know well, you'll have
that cat, body pressed down on the earth and fur
electrified, stretching her limbs for mercy.

ALWAYS TIME

There's always time for making love or
writing poetry – the two
activities revealing certain
parallels. Whether those stories
one has often heard are judged
as more amazing or amusing,
it seems no situation's ever
been too complex or unlikely
or ridiculous to stop
determined people.

Words or phrases sometimes come
with that same urgency, and minutes
open up, allow the time
to seize or lure them (whichever method
best achieves your purpose); tease them,
mouth them, use them every way
imagination leads, until
enough has passed between them and
yourself, and you feel sure there'll be
a further meeting.

Then, smoothing her hair and skirt,
straightening his tie, they go back to
their separate lives – return to where
he was before, what she'd been doing.
The prospect of a poem or
an assignation as secure
as such matters ever are –
only the time and place to be
arranged; minds already hard
at work and scheming.

THE FUNCTION OF TEARS

The function of tears
must be to serve as language,
a message to others —
yet the bitterest weeping
takes place alone. The message
then for oneself, an urgent
attempt to reach
that shackled prisoner
in the deepest dungeon
far below the level
of the lake.

What do tears express
that words cannot do better?
Tears are the first language;
a glazed face and anguished
moans communicate
rage, pride, regret,
pleasure or frustration,
remorse and hatred:
almost every emotion
sufficiently intense,
before words can be formed.

Each of these feelings
in turn must colour
the soul of the prisoner
abandoned in her corner,
like the shifting greys
tinged by rainbow hues
of light filtered
through tears clogging

her lashes, jagged
prisms of memory
and hope in the gloom.

Such tears have little effect
on the silent warder
who checks the links
of her chain, brings bread
and drinking water
and sometimes even
changes the musty straw.
No one has ever seen
the warder cry –
not his wife or children,
not the torturer.

Perhaps the lake
was hollowed out by tears.
But until the castle
is assailed, besieged,
completely undermined,
with dungeons flooded,
crenellations tumbling,
and torturer, warder,
. and prisoner are forced
to shout above the sound
of rushing water,

call to each other for rescue,
swim clear of the ruins,
embrace and cry with relief –
that lake, like the socket
of a giant eye drowned

by unimaginable
grief, will still stare
blindly up toward heaven
and go on weeping,
endlessly replenished
from a fountain of tears.

FIRE

Fire, like all servants, must be watched
continually. Fire, the best servant,
therefore the most dangerous.
Every servant dreams to usurp his master –
moved by the same ferocity as fire
rioting through tenements, incandescing
block after block of their pattern
(a chart lit up to demonstrate
the saturation-bombing – those who plot it
being fire's unwitting servants).

Once got loose, fire will eat metal
girders, cement structures, papery bark
of eucalyptus trees, household pets
or humans, consume anything. Because nothing
is alien to fire, as the perfect servant never
shows surprise at his master's demands. Contained,
fire can work miracles but, rampaging
free, reduces even his own hearth
to ashy desolation – then creeps back,
surly, to sit weeping in the ruins.

MY RINGS

On my right hand since then
I've always worn the ring
my father and I chose
as my twenty-first birthday present.
On my left, these months
since her death, my mother's ring:
the engagement ring he bought her
half a century ago,
and gave to me,
after the funeral.

The only break in his grief,
those first mourning days,
was when he learned
the two of them would lie
together under the same slab.
Ten weeks later, throttled
to death by a cancer, he followed.

If I forget . . . then let
the faded garnet oval
in its antique setting
tighten around that finger
like a garotte; the diamond,
angular, stab sharp
up my arm and pierce my heart.

I spread my hands on the desk.
Prominent tendons and veins
on the back, like hers;
red worn skin of the palm
that chaps and breaks
so easily, inherited

from my father. Even without
the rings, the flesh of my hands
is their memorial.
No need for anything
more formal. Not gold
nor platinum and precious stones
can serve as well
as these two orphaned hands.

QUESTIONS

How go on being angry with the dead,
remembering his mortuary face —
the chill when you bent and pressed your lips against
a substance no longer flesh: too cold, too dense;
the urge to take his body in your arms,
stretch out by his side — not believing any embrace
could warm him back to life, but simply a need
to lie with him there in the casket as though that
were your duty and pleasure. You wanted nothing else.

How go on being angry with the dead
when those last weeks of pain play themselves through,
over and over again — those sounds, those gestures.

The view from that room: luminous winter days.
The structure of a tree lit from every
angle. The setting sun sinking into
its cage of branches. After his death you lay down
on the bed to see exactly what he'd seen:
a glowing endless sky, flushed and tender.

Yet unaffected by these memories,
still that anger. Is it only anger
because he died — the rankling of guilt you share
with everyone alive toward their dead,
a ruse of the brain to survive the time of grief;
or is it a true and valid anger against
the ones who brought you into the world to die
but taught you nothing about how to die
and leave you with the questions unanswered.

THAT COMING MYSTERY

The longer you stare into its depths, the further
the fire recedes, the wider it spreads. Those knots
of heat, whirling eddies of light where the final
drops of sap lay hidden, untouched till now,
flare up, explode, as though a galaxy
were being born. Like staring into the eye
of a storm, when clouds are as turbulent as waves
beneath a cliff. If you look for too long at one
of these things it seems to surround you, and perhaps
for a moment you'll have the luck to become part of it,
to lose your separateness in the heart of whichever
element – in a water-bead, a flame,
the moving air, or rock and earth. What you watch
with such attentiveness is the breaking and re-creation
of matter's forms . . . That coming mystery.

SQUIRREL IN HOLLAND PARK

An after-lunch walk: autumn's first flaccid, fallen leaves,
canopied trees which held off the raindrops and filtered the light
Between trunks plaqued with moss the squirrels approached,
tails buoyant as brushstrokes, self-assured as spoiled children.

The most confident of them all was blind on one side,
orb dull, shrunken and white as the boiled eye of a fish.
With the other black, darting, totally alert eye
it judged the exact distance to reach the proffered nut.

Fingers and hair the same tarnished, chemical yellow as those
tense paws, when the man who was feeding it, clucking his tongue
and murmuring endearments, noticed me watching, with a confused
gesture he nodded and winced away, grasp tightening
on the crumpled paper bag. The squirrel stopped, and turned
its good side round to judge another likely patron—
who pulled the collar closer round her throat, kept moving
down the avenue, feeling completely unwanted.

HOSPITAL FLOWERS

Hospital flowers seem to last longer, or is it
only that they are kept longer, looked at
more often, share the same tainted yet
sustaining air until like us they are half-
drugged. Unless the nurses take them away,
day after day they wilt in regulation
vases or comandeered drinking glasses,
reminders of the friends who brought them
and that fear which, though omnipresent, looms
clearer here than in the world outside, the place
where flowers are forced for just this purpose.

Those fraying petals, having undergone
the entire process from glossy bud to insect-
like arrest, now resemble rare
aberrations waiting to be classified.
Tulip and iris, snowdrop and freesia succumb.
Carnations parch, anemones harden. The delicate
inner streakings fade and scent disperses.
As though wincing under a probe, narcissus,
jonquil and daffodil contract, twisting
around an invisible axis. Their trumpets
roll inward: visitors' crumpled sweet-papers.

Yellow and black of pollen powders my fingers
as I rearrange them, and the patterns of veins
marking their tissues, whose colours alter
inevitably as bruises, are like those on the limbs
of flushed, unconscious patients waiting
to be wheeled back to their darkened rooms. But

though stem and blossom may soften, fleshy leaves turn
limp and spongy, still they slope bravely as bullet-
frayed banners, torn trophy flags, or yesterday's bunting
half-bleached by the rain, after celebrating
the same old local victory again.

DREAMING

Night after night in that place
I see myself from above,
hunched over an open
book, and watch words form,
the empty pages crawl
with an alphabet of worms.

Only by a tremendous
spasm of will (almost
a miracle – as much as
must have been used to name
the world) can I create
the necessary words.

Fretful and restless as actors
paralysed on the screen
when the mechanism stops,
my characters wait, while speeches
and motives are imagined.
Then the story continues.

The plots are violent
and complicated, histories
of the tribe. Like a weary
scribe who copies an unknown
script from a blurred and doubtful
source, I wake exhausted

by this obligation
to think each thought and write
each phrase before I read it —
for no reward, with nothing
ever understood or
learned, and the dream gone.

USUALLY DRY-EYED

'Do you cry easily?' At times. Always
at what is called the cheapest sentiment.
Especially when lovers are reunited,
brothers reconciled, son safe and well
at home with his mother, husband and wife
smiling together. Those are the basic tales.

I'm moved to tears also when the hero wins through
and the siege is lifted, the message delivered, the years
of work rewarded – whenever modest virtue
is recognized. They are tears of pleasure
at the closing of the circle, when Heaven sinks
to earth and existence becomes ordered, just, and perfect.

And tears are brought to my eyes by any report
of natural disaster: when rains fail or fish
move away, devastation destroying the labour of hundreds,
sharp-tipped heel crushing the ants' nest.

But tears are not appropriate nor adequate
response to arrogance and cruelty.
Tears make one impotent. Anger is needed. Anger,
the activist. And anger must stay dry-eyed.

MEAT

This subject might be better for a painter,
a moralizing painter – the butcher's window
framing him: anachronistic whiskers,
ruddy face, white coat, striped apron, the sort
of tradesman one had thought no longer could
exist; and her: a proper Chelsea lady
of a certain age, hatted, necklaced,
mackintoshed, whose rouged and powdered cheeks
seem quite another substance than the flesh
of booted girls who stride along the pavement.

The gloomy afternoon accentuates
the disconcerting glitter of the shop:
refrigerator doors, refulgent tiles,
enamel trays displaying cutlets, kidneys,
liver, mince, scallops of veal, oxtails
and stewing steak – that close detail behind which
all the action will take place, and, as
a background (filling in for mountains, say,
or distant vista of a plain or lake)
hang carcasses made ghostly by their sheath
of creamy fat, and ghastly by the blood
congealing in their blackened, swollen veins.

He holds a tray of gobbets out for her
inspection almost deferentially,
as though the relics of a martyrdom,
some tortured part – and she bends forward, solemn,
thoughtful, curious. Two faces
from the crowd around the rack or headman's block.

I cannot hear, but guess he's vouching for
its authenticity. Each animal
received an individual injection
of adrenalin, to tenderize the flesh
with fear and rage. She's pondering, her vacant
eye reflective as a sphere of gristle,
intent upon deciding what to choose.
And in that chrome and crimson antiseptic
antechamber to the slaughterhouse, they
seem the natural focus of the composition.

THE KING MUST DIE

King of this once-splendid country,
now falling apart
beneath the blows of my most favoured subjects—
I know how he must feel, that wounded activist
hidden in a mountain village or
a room behind a garage in the suburbs.

This city, the capital,
stained by blood and noisy with explosions,
has been my heart and brain;
that mountain range the spine to hold me upright,
the river my bloodstream—
rocks and earth and sky as intimate
and vital as my own body.

Somewhere near the palace, in one of those ministries
whose flags are shredded with bullets, windows shattered,
walls plastered with proclamations,
the sons of murdered deputies
argue with their followers.
If this country is my body,
are they the cells that multiply with jungle energy
or my true doctors?

I have become just one more man amazed
and helpless as he learns the process of decay:
a miner coughing his lungs out (we are rich in metals),
a forester watching his leg mortify
where the saw slipped—or a woman after days of labour,
who feels the child refuse, her last blood pour away.

Like them, and my son's friends
(they tell me he has disappeared),
I know that I am dying with the country
I still love and call myself,
but have no power or wish to save.

THE NEW SCIENCE OF STRONG MATERIALS

(With acknowledgements to Professor J.E. Gordon, and the second edition of his book, The New Science of Strong Materials, *Penguin, 1976.)*

Plastic flow or brittle cracking:
whatever the material,
always the inescapable
potentiality within the structure
of either form of fracture:

these two failure mechanisms
are in competition for
all inadequate and earthly matter.
If it yields, the fabric's ductile.
Brittle, if at first it cracks.

Trying to visualize the three-
dimensional reality
of imperfection, dislocation's
vortex, the maelstrom of shearing, I guess
the faultlessness and ease with which

the rows of atoms can reject
the slightest deviation, yet not
acknowledge or accept even
a modicum of individual
involvement or decision.

They barely need do more than shuffle
one small fraction of an Ångström
in position, and quite soon
the incomplete half-sheet of atoms
has been edged outside. The others

have combined, closed ranks. Stresses
and strains, pressure and tension: the language
not only of engineering. Though
the combinations seem almost endless,
the basic elements are few,

their governing rules the same: just different
ways of dealing with dislocation
and stopping fracture, rare
recorded attempts and rumoured
success at cohesion, bonding, and union.

TO SOMEHOW MANAGE A POEM

There's a patched-up, incongruous neatness about his appearance
like a mongol child who's just had his collar buttoned and straightened
and a careless flannel rubbed across his face

Or the photo sent of a hostage, yesterday's newspaper
propped against his chest to prove he's still alive

Or that figure in the witness box, so pale and thin, who whatever
the consequence cannot control his grin—
happy to be out of the cellars, to see
other people after months of one ranting inquisitor—
though his smile reveals the missing teeth; soon
he'll start to say everything he was told, he'll reiterate

And the hostage's wary muffled voice, scratchily taped,
left at the pre-arranged place, will accuse all his colleagues

And the child will stumble over his age
and name, but somehow manage a poem.

from

Climates, 1983

I. FURTHER ... CLOSER

First day of the second half of another year.
Again the evenings will be shorter, mornings later,
the centre of the solar system further away.

This fear of being exiled further from the source,
trapped in the desolation of my own centre,
where frozen winter will be autumn's only harvest.

What could be further than my soul from any centre
of light and warmth and energy? If the sun is a jewel
in its creator's crown, his face is turned away.

But what horror, if he should swerve round and fix his gaze
on me. Nothing I was or thought could endure those eyes
as they came closer, and cauterized my darkest centre.

And yet I still keep moving closer to the furnace-
centre, that jewelled horror now as cool as water,
where he reigns, lord of all knowledge, where night and day

have the same length, winter and summer eternally stopped
at Heaven's equinoctial centre, closer toward
the promised revelation of his other face.

II. WHILE SUMMER RUNS ITS COURSE

Somewhere a few miles south or north
the sun is shining. Or closer still,
straight up, above the cloud, a brilliant
azure summer sky, unlike
this pallid swathing round the grey
church tower, asserts the actual season.
But here, a milky hush obscures
the day, and birds behave as though
it's almost twilight, not late morning.

Today this muffled noon conforms
well with my mood – it seems to promise
change (birdsong strengthens, blueness
curdles, shadows harden), yet
everything remains potential.
Later, if the local pattern
holds, the sky will clear and colours
throb and deepen into glory
just before the sunset chorus.

Or the day might end in storm,
piling clouds above the trees
that form a curtain closing in
the garden, and the birds go silent –
which would answer to another
aspect of my need: a sudden
rain to filter through the rocks
and roots and graves, be purified
into the universal water.

This year, while summer runs its course
and I attempt the furthest zones,
expose myself again to all
the different pressures and climates
of the past, I expect
to alter as often as the weather.
And if the sun and rain produce
their normal miracle once more —
perhaps I too shall come to harvest.

III. THE DISTANT VIEW

Summer rain
streaming down the window pane
is the sound of the wind,
and shaking trees,
heavy with their fullest leaves,
are the shape of the wind.

Ten years looking at the same scene,
the same tower, the same steeple.
Either the church is slowly sinking,
or the trees are growing taller.

Always the birdsong. The first
sound at dawn: pigeons
in the chimney, with the changeless message
of another morning.
And only the heaviest rainstorm
can drown for a moment
their mechanical calling.

Flaunting its burden of foliage
every branch and twig moves
in a different direction: thousands
of despairing gestures, an outdated style.
Inside the house, the silence—
except for wind, rain, birds—
makes such extravagant
expressiveness less viable.

Then, between showers, the flat grey sky
is stretched apart, coagulates
to cloud. The horizon returns. The trees
are calmer. Soon the sun will be setting.

Birds begin to celebrate
that blue and crimson certainty.
Everything looks smaller, clearer,
further away, and quickly, before
I lose the distant view and rain
comes down again I close the curtains.

IV. LIKE SHADOWS ON THE LAWN –

sentences form in my head
float in and out of my mind.
The thinner the cloud and stronger
the source of light, the firmer
the outline: a tentative smile
spreading across an unknown
face. The pale sky moves
above the empty garden,
and moods and memories
as seeming-motiveless
as this uncertain weather
follow each other, colour
my thoughts, then fade before
expressed by tears or words
or action. But that stranger,
with features so familiar
I might be looking in
a mirror, could determine
my future if I will
accept what she bestows,
and every shadow harden
wane and disappear
when noonday sunlight burns
away the morning haze.

V. ANOTHER VARIATION

Motor mowers, shrieking children,
and the slamming of car doors.
Sunday dinner smells. Summer
in the village. Soon the bells
will start. A stranger still, tonight
(as usual) I shan't go to the pub,
but stay here in my room. Then,
the only sound, after everyone
has gone back home and dogs have stopped
their barking, will be my own pen scratching,
matches striking, papers torn
perhaps as I reject another
variation of this poem.

VI. ANGEL FROM THE NORTH

Now, between July and autumn,
August makes its own season.
The clouds seem higher, piled in sharper
whites and darker greys, the sky
already colder – arctic tones
above the glowing apple trees,
laden with a better crop
than these ten years I've lived here. Next month
such rain would strip the leaves, every
morning raise another ring
of tawny mushrooms, mournful flocks
of martins gathering for their
long journey south. Today, the lawn
shows only greener and more livid
when the storm stops, and still the sun
strikes hot before a further bank
of cloud blots out the light, moving
like an angel from the north –
whose fiery sword of frost will bring
the apples down to rot among
the sodden leaves and faded grass,
and mark the garden like the first-born.

VII. VANGUARDS

Autumn begins with drizzle and the smell
of burning stubble. Though I shut all windows,
acrid smoke permeates the house.

That sound is not artillery nor rain,
but straw's dry crackle. Only from the attic
am I high enough above the garden trees

to see those black paths streaked across pale fields
where ash becomes the final harvest
and birds rise in alarm.

                  Later, at twilight,
that distant glow, orange and red, with its nimbus
of curdled white, could be a battle ground,

and every separate fire a gutted tank—
vanguards threatening a long campaign
of skirmishes as winter closes in.

VIII. AN UNMARKED SHIP

An unmarked ship, entering
the harbour of an undefended
town: autumn bears down on the land.
Driven by a north-west wind,
banks of cloud are the weight of sail
carried on its towering masts,

and that relentless grinding back
and forth of harvesting machines
across the fields becomes the distant
shouts for help and last attempts
of the inhabitants to save
themselves before the plundering starts.

IX. RED SKY AT NIGHT . . .

Clouds in horizontal bars
lit gold beneath, shaded mauve
above, with flame and scarlet centres.

Puce and dove become a pure
blue sky that deepens, heightens. Red
brick house, red roof-tiles, rose-hips

and crimson autumn leaves. And all of it
my delight, though I am more
one of the hungry flock than a shepherd.

X. ANTICIPATED

This month I've watched the moon through every change
from thinnest crescent into ripeness, from August
languor into clear September. Unseen
between two darknesses, full moon will be
tomorrow morning, just before noon. Tomorrow
night, hours after the unmarked climax,
her strength already waning, will be too late.
Tonight her energies are at their height.

Full moon used to awe me, craze me — now
I feel equal to her power. This
moment perhaps I too have reached an acme,
and the over-arching sky, the garden trees with
their rustlings and shadows, their nightingale-language,
are satellites circling around the centre
everything on earth anticipates
and this one night allows me to become.

XI. TO BREAK THIS SILENCE

Wind and trees and birds, this vague and always
changing weather – how they cut me off
from him with whom I share my house and life,
and I am altered by the seasons' power.

Hours each day together. Yet not enough
to counterweigh the glamour I succumb to,
those hours spent staring at the fire. It seems
that nothing happens but the rain and sunset,

night-mist curling through the hedges. The habit
of our mutual isolation forces
me to seek persuasive words to break
this silence – the key and explanation why

the radiance of a sphere of light against
the clouded autumn sky, swathing the moon
like fruit around its stone, confirms that we
have come to be the other's fate and climate.

PASSENGER

Not watching trains pass and dreaming of when
I would become that traveller, glimpsed
inside the carriage flashing past a watching
dreaming child, but being the passenger

staring out at tall apartment blocks
whose stark forms cut against the setting sun
and bars of livid cloud: balconies crowded
with ladders, boxes, washing, dead pot-plants,

into lighted, steamy windows where women
are cooking and men just home from work, shoes
kicked off and sleeves rolled up, are smoking, stretched
exhausted in their sagging, half-bought chairs,

under viaducts where children busy
with private games and errands wheel and call
like birds at dusk: all that urban glamour
of anonymity which makes me suffer

such nostalgia for a life rejected
and denied, makes me want to leave the train,
walk down the street back to my neighbourhood
of launderettes, newsagents, grocery shops,

become again that watching dreaming girl
and this time live it out – one moment only
was enough before a yawning tunnel-
mouth obscured us both, left her behind.

HERE

Here, like a rebel queen
exiled to the borderlands,
the only role I can assume
is Patience, the only gesture,
to fold my hands and smooth
my robe, to be the seemly one,

the only precept, always
to know the truth, even if forced
to silence, never to deny
my unrepentant nature.
I am my own tamer.
This life is the instrument.

And yet the iron hand wears
such a velvet glove,
and dreams and memories
of prelapsarian happiness —
simple actions which, when
first performed, lacked that content —

return to slow my steps
as I climb up and down between
the parlour and the kitchen
to fill my watering-can again
and give the plants their ration,
make me question that self-image.

Some power, created by
an altered vision, moving
to a different rhythm,
annihilates the past, revealing
space enough for another
universe. And there,

where needs and wishes synchronize,
where truth is changed and laws
revised, the capital has fallen
to a friendly tribe,
and I can leave this exile
when I choose, or rule from here.

STUBBORN

My Stone-Age self still scorns
attempts to prove us more
than upright animals
whose powerful skeletons
and sinewy muscled limbs
were made to be exhausted
by decades of labour
not subdued by thought,

despises still those dreamers
who forget, poets
who ignore, heroes
who defy mortality
while risking every failure,
spirits unsatisfied
by merely their own
bodily survival.

I know her awful strength.
I know how panic, envy,
self-defence, combine
with her tormented rage
because they will deny
her argument that nothing
but the body's pleasure,
use, and comfort, matters.

Guarding her cave and fire
and implements, stubborn
in her ignorance,

deaf to all refutation,
I know she must insist
until the hour of death
she cannot feel the pain
that shapes and haunts me.

OUTSIDE THE MANSION

As though we stood with noses pressed against the glass
of a windowpane, outside a mansion, dazzled
by the glowing lamps, the music and the circling dancers:

festivity, ceremony, celebration,
all equally alien to my sort of person.
Such a failing passes down the generations.

It could well be a fairy story, half-remembered.
I've often wondered if some godmother uninvited
to the party, vengeful, cast her mournful spell.

So profoundly known, the joyless spite spoilers
use to ease such pain; envy and disappointment
proudly claim choice of the unavoidable.

Stronger than the doubt of being right or wrong,
that denial is our sole tradition. We watch
the windows darken as the curtains slide across.

THE PRISM

Braided like those plaits of multi-
coloured threads my mother kept
in her workbox (beige, flesh, and fawn
for mending stockings, primary tones
to match our playclothes, grey and black
for Daddy's business suits), or Medusa-
coils of telephone wires, vivid
as internal organs exposed in their packed
logic under the pavement, nestling
in the gritty London clay,
associations fray into messages:

codes to unravel, cords to follow
out of prison, poems which make
no concession, but magnify
the truth of every note and colour,
indifferent whether they blind or deafen
or ravish or are ignored; the blueprint
of a shelter against the glare
– and the waterfall to build it near –
the perfect place to sit and hear
that choir of hymning voices, and watch
the prism of the rainbow spray.

ENTRIES

Like notes of music black against the stave,
the look of words and letters in purposeful
groupings, printed or written, seems to convey
a meaning more definite than their overt
message — even when understood.

But, thorns on the knotted stems of briars
thick as the hundred-year growth around the sleeping
princess, or a spider-web's decoration
(dried-up flies like November blackberries,
legs contracted in death), how well they hide it.

Dark beetles, swimmers with glistening backs,
etching their hieroglyphs between worm-casts and pebbles,
bird-claw cuneiform and rabbit-tracks
across dawn's snowfall, runic silhouettes
of trees upon the sunset-streaked horizon,
the icicles' oghamic alphabet,

each mark, spoor, trace, or vestige left,
every shadow that stirs the wheatfield
as if a god strode there, are the imaginings
and melody of energies beyond
control until expressed: entries
in the dictionary of another language.

OBSERVATIONS OF THE TOWER BLOCK

During the day the building becomes a gigantic machine
collecting data from the whole district. At night,
a Cunard liner with every cabin occupied,
rigging decorated for the final gala.

Different patterns of lights. No matter how late I go
to bed or early I wake, there are always lights burning.
Nights of insomnia, when I look out the window, someone
else who lives in that building is also not sleeping.

The lights glow pink and yellow, green and orange.
Is it from coloured bulbs, or filtered through curtains?
Who are the people who live in those apartments?

Illuminated lift-shafts, halls and balconies. Is it
the grid of the structure determines their lives? My sightings
are too irregular to grasp a pattern or meaning.

AUTHOR! AUTHOR!

What I am working at and want to perfect —
my project — is the story of myself: to have it
clear in my head, events consecutive,
to understand what happened and why it happened.

I wander through department stores and parks,
beyond the local streets, seem to be doing nothing;
then an overheard phrase or the way light slants
from the clouds, unravels the hardest puzzle.

It takes all my time, uses so much energy.
How can I live, here and now, when the past
is being unwound from its great spindle, and tangles
forgotten motives around the present? Rather

than set the record straight, further knowledge
complicates. I cannot stop the action
to make a judgement, or hope for better.
Every gesture casts a longer shadow

into the future, each word shifts the balance.
I see myself as one more character
in this extravagant scenario,
the story not yet finished. And who's the author?

SEDIMENTS

The moment the door closed, your smile fell like cigar ash
onto the carpet, leaving as little trace,
and once again alone, off-guard, worn out
by the party you had to work so hard at,

all that's left to do now is rinse out
the glasses and raise the window to air the place,
watch the brake-lights interweave their pattern
up the boulevard and throw the butts out,
pull the heavy curtains to then undress
and slowly clean the makeup from your face
while your brain keeps circling round that print-out
of what you meant but never got to say,

until the bath filled with its scented comfort,
and afterwards (the naked footstep marked
so clearly in the talcum powder spilled out
across the floor is like a castaway's)
you take the silver pill-box from your handbag
and wide-awake though tired enough to pass out,
lie down on the bed and feel the swirling
sediment dissolving in your veins.

SILK KIMONOS

Jade green and pale gold
under dark autumn cloud, worn flimsy
by rain and frost and wind – the planes'
leaves shift across their boughs
and the closed fronts of houses like silk
kimonos over dancers' limbs.

THE JOURNEY

Head against the glass, eyes close
to the train window, everything that grows
along the siding blurs and streaks: a green
and brown and yellow diagram of speed.

Not until I urge my gaze backwards
down the line can I distinguish saplings,
plumy grasses, flowering weeds and briars
sown there haphazard. Lifting my eyes higher,

one pigeon, pale against thunder-clouds,
spot-lit by a fitful summer sun,
rises above a formal wood, dense
trees all the same size, as though planted together.

Softened by the mirror of a tunnel,
my reflected face stared out, much younger,
superimposed like an old photograph.
If I sat opposite, one glance

comparing the two would be enough to inform
myself of every change that time has wrought.
Suddenly, I learned I was not other,
earlier, than what I have become

but only now am forced to recognise.
Wings beating it further up the sky,
to a bird's eye, the whole route is visible.
The nature of the country makes no difference,

nor the hastening traveller's confusion
(journey unended, memories unproved)
between conflicting versions of the legend
uniting images and questions

concerning fate and chance and fortune. Dazzle
of sunlight, then shadow, blinding me in the carriage.
A horse alone in a meadow, the level-crossing.
A steeple. The first houses. The train is stopping.

LAUNCHING

Autumn. Early morning.
A bench near the pond in Kensington
Gardens. This park is where
I've watched the seasons change
for twenty years. Under
my feet, yellow and crimson
leaves, colours as pure
as though with death their poisons
were purged; but further away,
against an empty sky,
the rusty foliage
of a shrubbery like a head
of hennaed greying hair.

Through the playground railings
the swings and slide and sandbox
I feared and hated. No one
told me how short such moments
were, nor taught the art
of living in the present.
There seemed so many dream-
scenarios. Now,
the only roles left: leathery
tourist, plastic-bag crazy,
literary lady or
admirer of grandchildren's
model racing yachts.

Spring and summer passed,
winter marking its own
bright blaze on what will not
endure, the balance shifts
from hope to human nature,

and the last self manifests,
poised for survival. But meanwhile
come days like this, when nothing
yet seems crucial, blue
and gold and calm, with time
to feed the ducks and learn
about finality, all
the different styles of launching.

AFTER FIFTEEN

to David

First there were close-ups: fallen petals,
patterned bark, fungus on stones,
a baby's pram – garden scenes.
The playground where, laughing and rosy-
cheeked, you waddled after pigeons
in your padded snow-suit; I,
another discontented mother
by the sandbox. All photographs
which seemed to need between three and six
feet. Then the focus shifted,
lengthened, changed. Now, Sunday
morning in the park, six feet
tall, you stand against the peeling
plane-trunk, look up through its leafless
twigs and branches, camera aimed
at pallid winter clouds. 'Fifteen
to infinity?' you ask, to confirm
the setting. Yes. You have grown
to become the photographer, and time
expands around you like the dizzying
crown of the tree and sky above:
fifteen to infinity.

LOVE-FEAST

Sulphur-yellow mushrooms like unlaid, unshelled eggs
inside a chicken's stomach when my mother cleaned it.
This morning, mushrooms on the lawn made me remember.

Bright as dew on the grass and silver with air-bubbles,
a stream of water splashed from the dull brass tap against
the side of the sink and over her red-chilled fingers when she
opened the carcass and laughed to show me how some were almost
ready – yolks only needing their coating of lime and mucus,
while others were still half formed, small as pearls or seeds.

Always, once the chicken was plucked and quartered and boiling
my mother would take those eggs, marked with twisting coils
of crimson threads like bloodshot eyes, and the liver put aside
on the draining-board in a chipped old china saucer, and fry them
with an onion to make our private treat. In the steamy
kitchen, the two of us would eat, and love each other.

HANDBAG

My mother's old leather handbag,
crowded with letters she carried
all through the war. The smell
of my mother's handbag: mints
and lipstick and Coty powder.
The look of those letters, softened
and worn at the edges, opened,
read, and refolded so often.
Letters from my father. Odour
of leather and powder, which ever
since then has meant womanliness,
and love, and anguish, and war.

WAR TIME

"Stand here in front of me," my mother said,
and pushed me forward in the downtown office
doorway. "Hide me." Behind my back she fumbled
with a sagging stocking and broken garter.

That garter: salmon-pink elastic crinkled
at the edges, half-perished, stretched too often,
it had lost the rubber button. Her stockings were
always too long. Something else to blame her for.

Her flushed face. My harsh stern eye. Of course
I noticed: the folded rayon top exposed
an inch or two of thigh — soft white flesh,
neglected, puckered with cold. (Another torment.)

Her round felt hat, pierced by a tarnished arrow
glinting in the drafty corner, bent low
as my ten-year-old shoulder, and the safety-pin
held between her lips seemed further off

than that umbrella-tip or those galoshes
of passers too distracted to ignore us.
No peacetime knowledge would assuage the future
we determined, one rainy winter morning.

OR HER SOFT BREAST

I could not get to sleep last night,
burning on the slow fire
of self-despite,

twisting on the spit that's thrust and
turned in such cruel manner
by my own hand,

until those earthy clinging arms
lifted out of the dark
to hold me fast

and drag me back to the same place
I thought I had escaped,
to see her face

as close as when I knew it first:
smiling, tender, perfect.
My fetters burst,

but the puzzle and the meaning
of my sudden freedom —
her touch on me,

soothing and cool, as though I sank
into a pool and drank
there, thankful —

was it a dream of love or death?
The grave, where I now slept,
or her soft breast?

LOST DRAWING

Bare winter trees in silhouette
against a clear cold turquoise sky
just after sunset: during the war,
at my aunt's house in Virginia, I tried
to draw them – trees like these in England
which she never saw – and now,
trees in my garden make me feel
the first true pang of grief since her death.

Between the washtubs and store-cupboards filled
with pickled peaches and grape jam, crouched
into a broken wicker chair,
I peered up through the basement window.
Sketchpad on my lap, with brushes and
bottles of black ink, blue ink, and water,
I wanted to convey the thickness
of their trunks, the mystery
of how a branch puts out a hundred
twigs, the depth and power of evening.

I heard her cross the porch, the kitchen
floorboards creak. As it grew darker,
that halo of light, outlining
all the finest intersections,
faded. Night absorbed the trees
the house the woman and the girl
into itself, kept every aspect
of that time alive, to give
me back today the memory
of my dead aunt and my lost drawing.

CRYSTAL PLEATING

for A. G.

Crystal pleating around the neck and shoulders
of that flamboyant crêpe dress I only wore once —
I remember the two of us shopping for it. Since then,
pushed into the back of the wardrobe, covered
with a dusty plastic, I've watched it fade
the way black dyestuffs do, to grey and copper-
purple, except those jetty streaks in folds
and hem. If mine now seems a witch's costume,
the queenly robe of silver-white you chose
must be all tarnished, should any part remain.
What a pair we looked. I knew how much
you needed me for a foil: the negative
of such a vivid presence, and I was glad
to serve your purpose. But my regard was not
enough, not what you wanted — and though the dress
would be quite perfect for a mourning garment,
I have not dared to put it on again.

THE STORM

Harry, I know how much you would have enjoyed it.
I can see your mouth's ironic curve as the heavens
opened. The umbrella over my head was almost
useless — rain and hail at the same slant
as your amused imagined gaze darkened
the side of my coat and trousers. Hard to resist
the thought that while we hurried back to the car
as soon as we could wait it out, cold
and distracted, someone up there was paying attention,
taking notice. The sky had been clear
enough as we drove through the cemetery
gates into those horizontal acres
ignored behind the bonfire sites and toolsheds
of surburban gardens, then parked and walked
between memorial stones to our appointment.
A spare man in a mac held the casket
chest-high as he approached. I stretched
a finger to touch a corner. The brass plate,
engraved with your full name, flashed paler
in the altering light as cloud thickened.

Cut into the piece of ground that was
the grave of both our parents — a square hole,
its soil piled nearby. A superstitious
qualm made me look down: too shallow
to disturb them. It must have been the very
moment the sexton stooped to put your ashes
there — where I hoped you'd want to be:
with them — that the storm broke. Instead of a struggle
with grief, we were fighting the weather, reduced
to the ludicrous; instead of prayer, a dry
shelter was what seemed most important. Water
running across my hands, inside my sleeves,

I took the spade and being chief mourner,
made the first movement to bury you. Harry,
I think you would have found the symbolism
too facile and pompous, and your sense
of humour stopped you taking it seriously –
though certainly delighted by the conceit
of Nature aghast and weeping at your interment,
my poor brother, her true and faithful poet.

IN MEMORIAM H.P.F.

God, the dead, the Donna Elvira
all inhabit the same realm:
the great democracy of Imagination.

Every paradise and underworld
beyond a blue horizon –
Sheol or Elysium –
is a beautiful product of mental function:
conjuration, prayer, and purpose.

I shall not meet my dead again
as I remember them
alive, except in dreams or poems.
Your death was the final proof
I needed to confirm that knowledge.

AS THOUGH SHE WERE A SISTER

As though she were an older or a younger
sister, whom I might bully, flout, ignore
or use, my dealings were not serious
enough. How could I think she was my sister?
What insolence — and luck, to dodge her well-
deserved rebuke. For she, more like a mother
(I the disrespectful child who shouts
and flails and pulls away) till now has not
abandoned or betrayed me. I must have seemed
ridiculous or worse to all who watched,
and most to those who recognized the Muse.

SPRING IN LADBROKE SQUARE

Embers still coated with ash,
these February buds — while others
already show the glowing nub
of life, each one Dionysus'
cone-tipped staff; and the first raw leaves
unhusked seem frail red curds and fibres
of flesh clinging to the twigs, as though
bacchantes had been here last night
to carry out spring's sacrifice,
and thrown the torn and bloody shreds
of Orpheus' limbs into the branches.

MARVELLOUS TOYS

*(with acknowledgements to Marcel Detienne &
Jean-Pierre Vernant)*

How was Dionysus captured by the Titans?
With marvellous toys: a cone, emblem of the goddess;
a pierced stone that roared like a bull;
a tuft of wool, like those his killers used
to daub on gypsum and disguise themselves;

a knucklebone, which grants divinatory
powers; a golden apple as his passport
to Elysium; and a round mirror
to see his ghostly other image – what child,
no matter how divine, could resist?

Who wanted Dionysus' death? Hera,
furious, had plotted to destroy him
in Semele's womb. Her malign advice
ignored, next she goaded Zeus to launch
a thunderbolt against the moony girl –

but the six-month child was sewn into his father's
thigh, for when the time arrived he must
be born. Yet wherever the boy was kept,
Hera's vengeful eyes pierced his disguise.
She sent her hit-men, the seven simple Titans.

What did the murderers do to Dionysus?
They cut his body into seven parts
which first they boiled and then they barbecued
(the ritual procedure) – but the heart
was put aside, to be saved by Athene his sister.

Why did Dionysus triumph? From
his beating heart, the vital central organ,
he was resurrected to defeat the Titans
(whose blood and ashes formed the human race),
to open the cycle of death and generation

and, horned like a goat or stag or ram, raging
over the mountains with his pack of Maenads and Satyrs
brandishing cone-tipped ivy-twined spears and tearing
apart whatever they met, to bring drunkenness
and madness: those marvellous toys of paradise.

TITIAN'S 'VENUS AND ADONIS'

He with that calculating look,
sated, half-rueful, of the local heart-breaker —
mustachioed garage-mechanic — and she,
the blacksmith's wife from further down
the square, mortified yet pleading:
why should he want to leave
all that lavish flesh and golden hair?

Even Cupid is asleep, drugged
by her perfumes and odours, his quiver of arrows
abandoned — but the dogs turn back to their master
and pull at their leashes, as though they sniffed
the waiting boar — and the plume in Adonis's
jaunty cap, stirred by the autumn
wind (perfect hunting weather,
sun pouring through thunder-clouds)
is equally restless. Nothing will thwart him.
Her insistence seems futile, his young
arrogance triumphant, and yet,
her power has never failed before.

SUSANNAH AND THE ELDERS

Sometimes she's painted clothed, though most
prefer her naked; she's shown at various
ages: a sturdy, angry girl
able to fight back – then more
submissive: flesh to eye and handle
by merchants choosing cattle, or ancients
hoping to revive their youth.

Often the elders are timid and crouch
under balustrades, hide in the bushes, peer
around statuary. But when the maidservants
leave her alone in the garden, emboldened
by lechery, the turbanned, scrawny-necked fools
creep to the foreground, pluck at her towels,
encourage each other with grimaces.

Yet no matter how passive she seems,
whether fearful, complacent or entirely
unaware of their presence, always
she inhabits a separate universe,
realm of living water and
indifferent good; inviolable
talisman of flesh and blood.

THE NOONDAY DEVIL

Demon of accidie, the noonday devil.
How well I know his power — he who besieges
the soul, slackens the hands and will, holds the sun
still, and makes each hour as long as fifty.

A bowl of lukewarm milk where flies settle:
my mind, subjected to these restless thoughts,
this weary languor — until I hate my work,
my room, my friends, myself and my ambitions.

Under his torpid spell my life seems endless:
fallow earth and unused, rusty plough,
a waterless cloud that never lets down rain,
a tree too often transplanted whose roots have withered.

Some days I can muster all my strength
for combat; others, just endure his torments.
But I have lost my hope in prayers and tears,
my appetite for anguish. Sloth always wins.

MIRIAM'S WELL
(*from Talmudic sources*)

On Sabbath evening, Miriam's Well,
and all its healing miracles –
that holy liquid which for her sake
saved the children of Israel, followed
them through the desert forty years –
moves from well to river, from river
to stream to well.
                    After her death
the flowing rock of Miriam's Well
sank in the sea, to rise again each
Sabbath and work its wonders. Miriam
died by a kiss from God. The Angel
of Death could not take her, nor worms
touch her body. When you draw the bucket
from Miriam's Well, if you want to hear
her prophesy, remember to fill
your mouth with water.

ARCHIVE FILM MATERIAL

At first it seemed a bank of swaying flowers
windblown beside a railway track, but then
I saw it was the turning heads of men
unloaded from the cattle trucks at Auschwitz.

THE MOUNT OF OLIVES

Eternity has staked its claim
to the hills around Jerusalem.
The dead have prime territory,
every slope a cemetery,
caves, crypts and catacombs
like ancient ovens hollowed
under olive groves and churches.

Cars and buses grind their way
below the Walls and up the valley.
Today, you are the only ones
who want to have the door into
the Sanctuary of Ascension
opened, the boy there told us. How
can I make a living without tourists?

Sitting on a rock beside
the Tomb of the Prophets, two men,
deaf and dumb, talk with their hands.
If across the Kidron Brook
the Golden Gate unlocked to let
Messiah through, and the resurrected
sang his praises, would they notice?

But still the dead ones sleep like babies
undisturbed by bombs, while above them —
rosy as cooks, stern as Crusaders,
pale as Hassids, watchful as soldiers,
silent as angels — spirits hover,
and Eternity settles deeper
into the land around Jerusalem.

LEONARD BASKIN'S DEATH DRAWINGS

I Death the Gladiator

He looks like the oldest gladiator left,
the only survivor from seasons of murderous games;
a pensioned-off mercenary from the border
campaigns, veteran of every atrocity.

Under the arena – those passageways
as complicated as the convolutions
of a brain exposed by primitive trepanning,
that warren of storerooms and cellars where animals
and slaves, weapons and chariots, are kept,
their walls of kidney-coloured brick rotten
with sweat of fear and pain – lies his kingdom:
trainer of the Colosseum's favourites.

II Death's Labour

Sated and exhausted Death,
head bent forward, heavy jaw
and scabbed bald cranium
a schoolroom globe marked with only
the largest seas and continents.

Sagging dugs, bursting thighs,
belly like a pregnancy
(womb which holds a universe
of unredeemable flesh),
gross and epicene, he's glutted,
stupified. Sick from over-eating
that eternal harvest of corpses,
he gags and vomits; gorged
beyond endurance, lowers himself
back as though onto a close-stool.

Eyes sunk deep in their sockets
(candles guttering out, choked by matter)
teeth worn down by endless grinding
of bones, nose corroded like an old
syphilitic's. But lax across
one knee, the bruised meaty hand
of a labourer. Death works hard.

III Death's Cloak

His fuscous wings could be a cloak
of ruffled feathers, incrustations
on an insect's carapace:

the chrysalis that broke to show
his arrogant incarnation
his evil glutted baby face

his massive and hairless torso:
the god whose cruel dilaceration,
limb from limb, no one escapes

as though for sport he thus torments
worms impaled upon his beak
summer insects in his busy hands.

IV Death With No Wings

It is the death you saw:
the tense hands of a wrestler
reaching out, the taut forearms
of a weightlifter, a prizefighter,
a porter from the meat market.

Nostrils like nares in a skull,
mouth a wound's torn lips,
tiny ears and eyes, head sunk
between the slab-slopes of his shoulders,
no neck. Great belly
and heraldic genitals.
Flesh pink-raw and hairless.

It is the death that comes with no pity
to thrust you into the charnel-pit.
Death with no wings.

V This Meat

This meat browning for our meal –
these charred woody fibres where
the seared surface seals and darkens,
clings to the pan, is what must have stuck
to the bars of St. Lawrence's grille
or the iron beds of Phnom Pen.
The sound flesh gave as the heat took
was unheard then through cries of pain.
Here in my kitchen, I am forced
to look and listen. I cannot ignore it.
This meat is the same stuff I am made from.
This meat I cook now for our meal.

TROMPE L'OEIL
(*at the Villa Farnesina*)

A blank niche in a wall
that you walk towards
with a vase in your hand
to place on the painted pedestal.
The pieces of broken glass
the bent stems
and fallen petals
and on the floor a pool of water.
Yourself putting them there.

THE ANGEL

Sometimes the boulder is rolled away,
but I cannot move it when
I want to. An angel must. Shall
I ever see the angel's face,
or will there always only be
that molten glow outlining every
separate hair and feathered quill,
the sudden wind and odour, sunlight,
music, the pain of my bruised shoulders.

RED MESSAGE

Stern ancestors, with features as intricate
as Japanese print-makers' seals or circuits
of transistor-cells. Wherever you lived,
flesh and bone of the clan became that place;
lives gone into the earth like water
poured for ritual, or dark ash strewn
from a sacrifice. Programmed by return
and repetition, watching the changing pattern
of smoke and sparks and leaves made time
another code to break: a white cataract
crashing over the head, or flames transmitting
their red message from the funeral pyre.

SPRING IN THE CITY

Petals from the trees
along the street
revolve and fall.
Complex currents
lift them up toward
the boughs from which
their flight was launched.

All the space between
the rows of houses
in swirling movement
like sand in a rock-pool
as the sea sluices through
raising fine clouds
that blur its clearness.

Gutters choked with blossom
pavements patterned
the wind-blown hair of girls
tangled with blossom
a swarm of insects
aquarium of fishes
snowflakes in a storm.

Shaken by the breeze
and cornering cars
reaffirming the spiral
of the galaxies
the air today seems thick
with stardust and we
are breathing stars.

ACROBATIC FULL MOON

A fat but agile acrobat
from a Chinese circus, the moon contracts
and elongates, then flattens out
again, making jokes with the clouds.
Or is it more a double-jointed
golden cat glimpsed between
gloomy jungle ferns, an orange
segment, an apricot-coloured egg yolk
slithering across the oily
surface of a frying pan?

Watching it pretend to be
a car's headlamp, the smiling face
of a Michelin-man, cloth cap worn
at a rakish angle, I almost thought
that a flower-pot of geraniums
nodding their heads in the pre-dawn wind
further down the empty street
was someone else still awake
leaning out to contemplate
the antic moon's variations.

Now at five o'clock this morning
standing in the same corner
to brew myself a cup of coffee
where every evening, cooking dinner,
I look westward through the window
toward the sunset, I can see
the full moon slide behind the trees
and blocks of flats, to vanish as
the room lights up behind my back —
heralding the next act.

VALLEYS AND MOUNTAINS

What I know are valleys
between the mountains
have buried beneath them
the crests of other mountains,

and I can see through depths
of stormy ocean
the drowned empires
there before the ocean,

trace the cool fern's pattern
in burning coal,
ancient sunlit
jungles become black coal,

and proving every tale
concerning love's
transforming power,
surely this must be love.

PASSIONS

Let's not mention love. It's like a glowing
stove to someone covered with burns already.
And hate is that dark cave whose depths conceal
a reeking oubliette where rivals groan.
One glimpse enough to turn your head
and make you lose your balance, envy will have you
spiralling from the top of the cliff, down
onto the breakers. Anger is the sea.
Gasping and buffeted, no matter how
you struggle or plead for mercy, you drown. But pride
can clothe those shattered bones with perfect skin,
and breathe into the lover's mouth her song.

NATURAL HISTORY

—then you captured my distracted spirit,
called it down from where it danced and hovered
above our heads, brought me back to myself,
trammelled by your gross and loving grasp,
into the realm of our own natural history,

into that garden where the flowers strain
on bristling stems toward the sun and arch
their petals wider, and the snail's slime-trail
stops at a broken shell as the harsh triumphant
beak stabs over and over through its pulpy heart,

where sounds and smells and colours, taste and touch
of hair and flesh, glistenings, swollen
heats and tension, matter's prodigal
and irresistible excess, all
transform the butterfly into a rutting primate.

THE MUSIC

I sit alone in my room
on a cold summer afternoon
upstairs from where you in your room
are playing the gramophone.
Though you don't know it, I open
my own door wide enough
to share the sound of the music.

Another floor up, in the attic,
two adolescent lovers
play a childhood game, just
rediscovered. Laughs, and the rattle
of dice, drift down from above.

Barely more than their age,
hidden on the steps below
the next-door villa, whose stones
still held the heat of day,
my head on your shoulder,
we listened to someone
playing the same tune.

That night, we hurried home
to our new games — perhaps
your memories are the same?
Or else, I have to wonder
why you chose the music.

DEATH'S LOVE-BITE

A slow-motion explosion is what my mouth's become,
front teeth thrusting forward at impossible angles.
Incisors once in satisfactory alignment
cruelly slice through lips and tongue, and molars grind
each other into powder. Though it took almost thirty
years for them to drift so far apart, the pace
accelerates. My mouth contains meteors
and molecules, the splintered bones of mastodons,
galaxies and Magellanic clouds; feels like
a photograph of particles halted in
a cyclotron and magnified a thousand powers,
a microscopic re-enactment of the planet's
coming total fracture, elements dispersing
out in space. That's the truth I clench between
my jaws, behind my face. And all the technical
ingenuity called upon to solve
this dental problem won't heal Death's love-bite.

CALCUTTA

Carts loaded with sacks and planks
moving into the pre-dawn city.
One man in front between the shafts,
two pushing from the back.

Knees drawn up to the chin,
rickshaw-men asleep
on the poles of their vehicles.
Black crows roosting.

A five a.m. sweeper,
stiff-legged, stooping
at an empty crossing
by the silent kiosks.

The gaunt fronts of hospitals,
their windows bright
as strings of coloured lights cascading
down this wedding pavilion.

And now the hired car goes past
another drug-store, another clinic,
the Panacea Laboratory,
another sweet-shop.

Dark brick obelisks and pyramids
along the ruined paths:
'. . . guide on, young men, the bark
that's freighted with your country's doom,'

Derozio's memorial,
and Rose Aylmer dead
in the Park Street cemetery.
Blood and marigolds at the Kalighat.

Give that girl thirty pice
because she's singing.
But don't look at the lepers'
blunted fingers.

In the Tibetan Restaurant, drinking gin,
middle-class intellectuals
to whom the greatest insult
is to be accused of pity,

and out at Dum Dum airport,
rising above the burning cow-dung pall
that blurs the skyline, another tourist
who can't take any more.

THE CIRCLE

We did not meet that often: once
or twice a year for drinks, or walking
to the store we'd stop and talk –
she the village dowager,
I the foreigner who'd stayed
a while but then decamped, become
one of the weekend people. Always
I admired that upright stance,
gallant style, and undiminished
presence. She still could play the perfect
hostess: draw me out about
the house, the garden, and the children,
and not touch on the personal.

But the last time – I was crossing
the far orchard, taking a short-cut
to the river – she called me over
to join her and the dogs, I noticed
something different. Those fine
eyes never were so bright
before, nor cheeks so gaunt and flushed,
hair disordered, gestures bewildered.
I started to say the usual things
about the weather and crops but
almost peremptorily, was
interrupted and asked, 'Tell me please,
do you enjoy fairy stories?'

It was the end of summer. I
remember watchful apple-pickers
as we paced back and forth between
the trees and she described the pleasure
of rediscovering old tales;

how I wanted to believe
that, like a circle closing,
connexion had been made from past
to present. Months later, a bitter
April day, I hear the news.
The circle was a fairy-ring,
as false as fairy gold, and nurses
guard her from worse bewitchment.

THE POWER SOURCE

In this part of the country
all through July, sometimes
round the clock, after
the first crop's cut and stacked,
the rape-seed brought inside
that new blue corrugated
plastic barn behind
the churchyard, the driers keep blowing.
Industrial farming. Often
annoying, ignored, it fades into
the background: one more factor
in the ambient pattern of sound.

I can let it lower my guard
and mood – becoming sulky,
agitated – or get me
high on the idea of progress:
a theme to brood on. Either
way, stimulated or
nerve-racked, I find the summer
different than before
I noticed the strain of trying
to be a nature-poet
these unbucolic days.
The power source has shifted.

When it stops, though other
motors seem much louder:
passing tourist traffic,
helicopters spraying,
tractors (drivers earphoned
to muffle their own noise),
the vital note is missing.

I wait its starting-up,
knowing I'll be uneasy
in the interval
between now and the August
combine-harvesters.

JUDGEMENT AT MARBLE ARCH

Office girls doing their lunchtime shopping.
Bewildered blond families up from the provinces.
Africans, Arabs, Italians and Spaniards.
Cut-price teeshirts, blue jeans and haversacks.
Oily exhaust fumes and noisy rock music.
Hot August sunshine, then the first autumn shower.

Just past Lyons' Corner House,
near Marble Arch Underground station,
I heard a low but penetrating moan
by my right shoulder, and turned to confront
a tangle of greying hair not quite concealing
eyes squeezed shut and open mouth (saliva
stretched in threads between the drawn-back lips)
of a woman – about my size and age – wailing
her distress. Her naked goatish legs
in heavy shoes kept stumbling forward,
somehow avoiding all obstructions.
The large red plastic bag in her dirty hands
was held as though at any moment she
would cover her head to hide from the assault
of sound and sight, or use it to vomit in.

Someone else had noticed – a caring friend
and wife and mother, I would guess.
Our doubtful glances intersected. Both
relieved from having to make a decision,
but wondering whether – the other a witness –
we were now committed to action, as well as pity
and horror. Slowly, through the midday throng,
we followed after, murmuring our uncertainty.
Whenever I got close enough to hear,
she was still mouthing her fear and curses.

The woman with me seemed as nervous.
'I'm frightened,' I confessed. 'Me too.'
Bright brown eyes stared back, grateful.

At Edgware Road a man reached out
to touch her arm. She had become visible.
The circle of watchers broadened.
She flinched and dropped,
then stretched the plastic bag across her face
as though it were a magic hood,
the fluttering red wings of a wounded bird,
a shaman's regalia with its tawdry glamour.
'Where's a policeman?' my companion muttered.
I had to get away. 'I'll try to find one.'

In another story I'd take her home
and nurse her, heal her, be a holy martyr.
But I didn't want to;
nor did I want to hand her over.
When I returned from where I'd stood
around the corner in a hotel entrance
the crowd had scattered. 'She crossed the road.'
Her voice had changed – alarmed, perplexed, almost
indignant. 'There might have been an accident.'
'Maybe she's been like this for years,' I mumbled,
ashamed of myself. 'So many sick people
in the cities . . .' 'Perhaps'.
For the first time we had to deal with each other
(if we talked longer, might be forced
to make a judgement), so said a brusque goodbye
and went back to our separate errands.

THE FUTURE

The future is timid and wayward
and wants to be courted, will not
respond to threats or coaxing,
and hears excuses only
when she feels secure.

Doubt, uproar, jeers,
vengeful faces roughened
by angry tears, the harsh
odours of self-importance,
are what alarm her most.

Nothing you do will lure her
from the corner where
she waits like a nun of a closed
order or a gifted young
dancer, altogether

the creature of her vocation,
with those limits and strengths.
Trying to reassure her,
find new alibis
and organize the proof

of your enthralment and
devotion, seems totally useless —
though it teaches how
to calm your spirit, move
beyond the problem's overt

cause and one solution –
until the future, soothed now,
starts to plot another
outcome to the story:
your difficult reward.

from

The Knot, 1990

THE KNOT

One of them showed me how to split a reed
and plait it into a holder for my hammock.
'When you know you've got to get away,' she said,
'use this piece of cloth, faded red, and knot
it tight at either end. Find somewhere far
from the children and dogs and vague old people,
the women thumping grain, those noisy men
around the smoky fire. Loop it under a branch
or over a beam in one of the empty huts
at the edge of the clearing. Then crawl inside,
when you need to be alone to hear the story,
the story you tell yourself all day but sometimes
cannot hear.' And sometimes, there in my hammock,
words would come and cluster together like wasps
between the poles and matting of the roof
as black as rotting fruit or drying membrane,
a blossom of words in a dusty ray of light.
Words would form a knot and start a story.

THE EUROPEAN STORY

I

A story? There's not enough action —
just an endless loping
through the cobwebbed aisles and arches
of a Gothic forest unreeling
like a painted backcloth. Then he stumbles,
and the heart in the cup of his bloodied palm
bounces into the ferns.

Red-cheeked, rawboned, black mustachioed,
a puppet escaped from its master, a soldier
on the run, he served the story's purpose —
did the murder, cut her open.
Now he doesn't matter.
The heart becomes the drama's centre.
Its voice calls out: 'My son, my son,
have you hurt yourself? My dear, don't fall!'

II

My mother might have told that story.
Cave-crone guarding the fire-spark
as safe inside its ball of clay and moss
as an infant lapped by womb-water,
she handed on the ancient curse
(the lesson I refused to learn)
mother-tongue mumbling heart-words.

Last breath from an open mouth,
moisture beads the fluttering threads
spiders wove between the branches
and makes a nimbus of splintered light
through tear-clogged lashes, a pearl-encrusted

iconostasis of wonderworkers
to prove Death weaker than Mother-love,
and reconcile the sacrificial daughters.

III

I was born in a smothering caul,
a veiled woman. My first cry was a protest.
I feared the antlered maskers' shadows
the rooting goddess who eats her farrow
the touch of Balder's frost-burned mistletoe.
In dreams I was the puppet-killer,
her defender, with sword and dagger sharper
than the Angel's, armour brighter than Joan's.

I have danced as either partner
been tormented and tormentor
but could not find the right disguise
to fool her – neither child nor mother
with my child. Oh what grief, never
to hear that special note in her voice:
'My son, my son, have you hurt yourself?'
You want to plunge the knife in your own heart.

IV

Cast your bread on the waters.
But the Old Man of the Sea
rises up and straddles your shoulders
tightens his grip on your windpipe.
There's salt in your mouth.
He's wet and cold and heavy.
You stagger and almost drown.

Then up from the ground between your feet
another one comes
and splits you open

thrusts his hand in the shambles
wrenches out your heart.
When he stumbles and drops it, the heart
cries out, My dear, don't fall!

V

A fish appears with a ring in its mouth
and three questions. An old woman
asks for shelter. If you pass the test
each wish is granted until the last

unless it is
to break the mould,
open out a parchment scroll,
cherubim and gargoyles
twining down the margins
throstles perched on gilded letters
leafy plants and scaly dragons,
and let the variations flourish;
to change the definitions
of feminine and masculine,
son & mother, love & duty,
and that final one, 'The End':
tell the story different every time.

VI

Change the heart into a ticking bomb,
the soldier to a girl — a terrorist,
the very last Crusader,
sure that a dark annunciation chose her
to save the Holy Places of the planet
by casual explosion.
That moves the story on.

Her ideas and actions must be examined
as carefully as a bomb's fuse and circuit,
with the tender skill a surgeon uses
cutting live flesh to open up a heart.
She has been formed by what the story means.
It started in Europe. It spread like radiation.
There's no immunity to images.

ON THE THEME OF ARTIFICE

'Himself, may be, the irreducible X
at the bottom of imagined artifice.'

What does Wallace Stevens mean? I've pondered
those lines, tried to decide if the imagined

always must be artificial – mind's
construction upon, and against, Nature, which he

projects into a pineapple that looms
gigantic as the jar in Tennessee.

* * *

It seems a form of magic: the poet artful
enough to draw the essence of reality

like a shawl, cobweb fine, through a golden ring,
or coax, from its constraining bottle, the genie

who surges to a mushroom cloud. The same
thought that split the atom, had to imagine

its irreducible nucleus
and the artifice of Time and Space, first.

* * *

At the bottom of imagined artifice,
rather than familiar gods and demons

or current versions of total destruction, he
himself is dreaming pineapples and jars.

THE YELLOW PLATE

i.m. A.G.

A painted plate, yellow-glazed below
the shallow curve of its white porcelain rim,
(yellow I'm always drawn to:
the saffron robe of a mendicant
     or the silk curtains a friend bought in Burma,
     mine now, because she's dead),
is the yellow road of the sun—
that bright furrow plowed between the stars.

Underneath is the painter's complex square mark,
lacquer red, and round scarlet stickers reading:
'Chia ching' and '1796 to
1820'. On the front, twelve creatures.

It took a long time to see
they were the Chinese zodiac,
animal, bird, and reptile, real
or imagined (the one in the center
is a dragon, not a crocodile),
that give names to the hours of the day
and the little twelve-day cycle,
the months of the year and the sixty years
I guess was the expected life span
of those hunters and shepherds.
     When she died, my friend was younger.

Tradition has it that Tajao, a minister
of Emperor Hwang-ti, circa
2697 B.C., invented them.
So little has changed since, the same
names are still used, (though I can't compute

what our year is by that calendar,
nor my own sign), and I sensed before
I knew what they meant and were.

The colors are green and red and yellow —
jade, cinnabar, and sulfur,
the drawn line blackish sepia.
A pale wash of pink fills
the bodies of the wrinkle-snouted pig
and the rat, whose ideograph is 'water'.
Too anxious for the luxury
of variation the rabbit is pure white.

Cloudy patterns blotch the horse,
whose mane and tail fall fine and soft
as new-washed hair, and the bristling dog,
like shadow dappling windblown corn.
Flamy stripes unite the horned sheep and
the thoughtful tiger biting a raised paw.
Dragon and serpent are scaled, checkered
and barred, their dangerous twirling tongues
high-voltage warnings.

The hen looks fierce as a cock, crested
and hook-clawed, not domestic
and submissive like the ox
with a rope through its round nostril.
The monkey has delicate hands, subtle
lips, and watchful eyes — a courtier
wondering if he's telling the right story.

Everything about the plate – all
the moods and colors, characters and patterns –
    she was like all of it,
    as beautiful.

FLOWER FEET

silk shoes in the Whitworth Museum, Manchester

Real women's feet wore these objects
that look like toys or spectacle cases stitched
from bands of coral, jade, and apricot silk
embroidered with twined sprays of flowers.
Those hearts, tongues, crescents and disks, leather
shapes an inch across, are the soles of shoes
no wider or longer than the span of my ankle.

If the feet had been cut off and the raw stumps
thrust inside the openings, surely
it could not hurt more than broken toes, twisted
back and bandaged tight. An old woman,
leaning on a cane outside her door
in a Chinese village, smiled to tell how
she fought and cried, how when she stood on points
of pain that gnawed like fire, nurse and mother
praised her tottering walk on flower feet.
Her friends nodded, glad the times had changed.
Otherwise, they would have crippled their daughters.

POPPIES

A bed of them
looks like a dressing room
backstage after the chorus changed costume,

ruffled heaps
of papery orange petticoats
and slick pink satin bodices.

Every petal's base
is marked with the same
confident black smear as a painted eyelid

and the frill
of jostling purple anthers
sifts a powdery kohl that clogs the lashes

shading watchful glances
from dilating pupils, as though
all the dancers swallowed belladonna.

The pleated velvet star
at the centre of each flower
is the top of a box filled with jet beads.

The hard green buds
are their husbands' fists, the silver-
bristled leaves are their admirers' beards.

FLIES

November sun as warm as a Levantine
winter made me push my window up
this morning, brought back donkey-drivers' calls,
the look and smell of bakers' stalls and offal
butchers. (Flies were everywhere.)

But the shudder of glass (fear a splintering shard
might pierce me) from the frame carelessly jammed askew,
as heavy lorries brake and lower gear
to take the corner for a shortcut to the A40,
changed those images to Home County:
a pan of clarifying sugar syrup
on the Aga wrinkling as it starts to boil
(the crab-apple jelly-bag dripping draws flies
to the kitchen), or the irritable twitch
of a horse's flank to shift the biting flies.

The noise I heard could have been
the drone of a distant combine harvester,
a helicopter spraying, or closer still,
here in town, a treadle-machine next door
(that new family must be tailors) and their
muffled hullabaloo through the party wall (they're
killing each other: the flies are driving them crazy).

So I went to put the window down, to stop
the thrumming and its associations, and found
summer's last fly, trapped by the double-glazing.

EARLY RIVERS

This jar of rosy-purple jam is labelled
Early Rivers, August '82 —
the date I made it, the name the farmer gave
those plums, smooth as onyx eggs, but warmer.

The dimpled groove, bloom-dusted, down each fruit
pouted at the touch of my knife, yielding
the stone I put inside a cotton sock
(relict of a worn-out pair — every
boiling dyed it darker crimson — from one
plum-season to the next I saved it) then pushed
the lumpy tied-up bag into the centre of
the pulpy amber halves and melting sugar
in the preserving kettle, and let the mixture
ooze its pectins, odours, juices, flavours,

until the chemistry of time and fire
produced this sharpness, sweetness, that I'm eating
now, straight from the jar, smearing my mouth,
digging the spoon in deeper, seeking a taste
undiluted even by nostalgia.

AUGUST

August is like a woman who's already thinking
that she'll soon be forty. There's something old-fashioned
about her, emanating a womanly odour
of sachets. You can tell that she's been badly treated
by men. Her daughter has left home. She's probably
divorced. She's the manageress of a dress shop.

One might talk of her carriage: she seems to be wearing
a corset. She's quite large and very white skinned.
Her hair is set, her face is powdered matt, and her
thin and rather mournful little mouth with lips
firmly closed on each other except when she bites
them, is carefully painted and always looks wet.

August is the month when everything stops growing.
She feels she stopped growing a long time ago; though
she wouldn't put it like that. She doesn't believe in
too much introspection. Dignified and solitary,
she walks through the park after work, under
the heavy, dusty, dying green of August trees.

THE NEVILLE BROTHERS
(at Vanderbilt University, Nashville, Tennessee, Spring 1985)

As soon as he walked on stage, I saw
that the lead singer was Lord Krishna
wearing a sleeveless red teeshirt, jeans
and high heels. He was gorgeous. In the dim
blue exit lights of the auditorium,
adoring him, we were all milkmaids.

I'd bought pictures of faces like his, full cheeked,
almond-eyed, from Bombay street vendors.
Just this side of fat, those shoulders
and pectorals for the moment are perfect.
A lush male torso slowly swayed
as nervous legs pranced and pawed like a horse.

Amplified drumbeats were driving them wild.
How often before he had watched tranced
devotees or dawn dancers wanting
more and louder, like the audience now.
But this was a concert on campus, not
the Juggernaut temple, or a bar in New Orleans.

Note: A New Orleans rhythm and blues group. Krishna grew up among a group of milkmaids who were entranced by the sound of his flute. He is worshipped in the form of the Juggernaut at the temple at Puri on the Bay of Bengal.

IN TUSCALOOSA —

a puppy trotted down from a verandah
past the yard-sprinkler, and led me to
the corner of an avenue
where oaks were swagged with mauve wisteria.

Breathless and excited as an orphan
I watched a misty nimbus form
around the streetlamps and glowing from
windows of houses where I knew no one.

OUT ON THE PORCH

Who expects the whole bus-queue
she passes while shopping,
like a chorus of gossiping aunts and neighbors
or the row of sunflowers, obediently heliotropic,
shading the porch where they sit and watch her,
to forget everything else, wishing her luck?

Whose neck stiffens and spine arches
trying to do what they want (she can't be
that much younger, yet still feels débutante),
desperate for approval.
It makes her eyes itch with exasperation—
like saying a poem for the aunts and neighbors

then later, from an upstairs window, hearing
that tolerant laughter out on the porch
over clinking teacups and impatient slaps
at mosquitoes as they change the subject.
Who insisted? Who arranged it?
Thank God when the bus comes.

OFF THE INTERSTATE

Following instructions
we stopped at every viewpoint
around the Painted Desert.
Mineral deposits
streaked like bird-droppings
over faded purples,
bled-out pinks and reds.
It looked like a crater filled
with cooling clinker under
rainclouds that might have been
smoke from its last eruption.

At the Petrified Forest
an elderly man in the car-park
started to talk about Jesus,
and the Day of Judgement
which was coming soon.
He wouldn't leave us alone.
Not even a downpour enough
to deter him. I kept busy
with my camera while he
invoked the four horsemen
to a mystified Japanese girl.

Hard to find the motel
Rosemary recommended.
We had to double back
to the last exit, where streamers
fluttered over gas-pumps.
Turning from the highway

toward the horizon – the sky
was perfectly clear now, golden
with sunset – there seemed nothing else
but the wind and rolling Coke cans
between me and the North Pole.

BOUZIGUES

There's a place on the road
coming down from the hills where rows
of oyster frames unfurl
on an indigo sea
like a pattern of bamboo fans
or blocks of pale embroidery
on a geisha's kimono—
whose knees and shoulders
press against the border
of the wood engraving
tight as Alice's
when she started growing.

The high-piled mass
of the dead volcano cone
is her oiled and twisted hair
fighting free from its combs
to tangle in the shell-
encrusted poles. Her eyes
look crazed. A small tooth shows
between pursed lips, and one breast's
tip in the oyster scent
of watered silk's
loosened folds. Her mood is
storm clouds over the lagoon.

Note: A village on the Bassin de Thau, on the south coast of France, famous for
its oysters. The lagoon is closed at each end by the extinct volcanic cones of Sete
and Agde.

BLOSSOM AND TECHNOLOGY

I wasn't sure what to expect,
after flying for eighteen hours
over the Pole. Japan
was contradictory images:
stone and technology,
crowds and cherry blossom.

I came too late for the blossom,
the one sight I did expect,
as if technology
could slow seasons and hours
till certain images
confirmed: this is Japan.

Some things were strange in Japan:
not the imitation blossom,
but those plastic images
of meals you might expect
in restaurants. The hours
to make them, the technology!

An older technology
had created another Japan
where no count was taken of hours
spent training flowers to blossom
in a place you wouldn't expect,
or painting a screen with their images.

I wanted to keep those images.
My camera – technology
of the sort I came to expect
from anything bought in Japan –
was aimed at every blossom
and stone as it changed with the hours.

I stood and watched for hours
near the temple images
people's faces blossom:
prayer's technology
must be what fuels Japan,
which is not what you'd expect,

nor expect that so few hours
in Japan could reconcile images
of blossom and technology.

THE JAPANESE BATH

I feared my heart would stop: the depth and heat
of water in the wooden tub, the thought
that even if I called you would not hear
from where you sat, beyond the anteroom,
silk-kimono'd by the painted screen.
I stretched my legs out, saw my body small
as a court lady of Kyoto, green
as moss around a temple garden pool
carp-filled, and how the same droplets of steam
frosting my hair beaded the darkened walls.
The silent isolation made me feel:
to come this far and drown could be foredoomed.
Then I stood up, showered off the dream
and ghosts with cold water, calm now, released.

JAPANESE SYLLABICS

When the tea-master's disciples praised
Kobori Enshu's beautiful scrolls
and plates, saying that no-one could help
but admire them, he sorrowfully
answered: 'This only proves how common-
place I am.' His dissatisfaction
at their response quite opposite to
my constant need for reassurance,
my placatory smile – the nodding
head-piece of a jointed wooden doll,
agreeing, agreeing.

              Legend tells
how he built the Katsura villa
on the following conditions: no
limits on money or manpower
or time, and no-one to disturb his
conception of temples and gardens
and pavilions by seeing the work
until finished. He was so secure
in his judgement, knew what he wanted.

Each gesture and implement exact,
the simple tea-ceremony is
a junction of choices, decisions;
its purpose (or am I imposing
an alien system of values
and totally misunderstanding?)
to enact and confirm the balance
calmness and grace I yearn for and lack.

Yet even such a grand tea-master
could doubt his purity of motive,
lament a lack of courage, wonder
whether his most precious treasure had
been chosen more to please others than
because it was to his own taste.

                                    Now
I'll show you my favourite puppet:
black brows, white face, and fluttering sleeves.
Her expression is so subtly drawn,
the painted features seem to change with
my opinions. But when she's being
praised, or when I'm confident enough
to stop equivocating, then how
balanced, graceful, calm we both can seem.

Note: Kobori Enshu (1576–1647) built the Katsura Rikyu in Kyoto for
Toyotomi Hideyoshi, exacting the three famous conditions.

INCENSE

A dull shine like black ice:
the bronze urn at the top of the stone steps,
its incised pattern the same pale colour
as the ash that fills it – from how many
millions of burned-out incense sticks?

Shiomi told me I could light one
if I wished. I watched the other mourners
pass their hands through the swirling smoke,
smooth it over their heads and waft
it down the fronts of their kimonos.

The red tips of the incense sticks
pulsed and glowed in the shadow of cedar
pillars and temple roof-tiles as I bent
close, murmuring prayers and names,
half a world from where they lay,

yet certain they were here with me,
supportive spirits among this strangeness.
The shrine doors swing shut in the wind
and the incense billows. Three women
laugh as though it means good luck.

KEEPER

Mother's fur coats,
silver teapot and velvet
boxes of broken earrings.

Aunt Ann's crackle-glass lamp
with its patterned parchment shade,
her mahogany bookcase.

Daddy's volumes of Jewish Thoughts,
A Hermit in the Himalayas,
those plaid plus-fours.

A faded suitcase, corded,
the sort a schoolboy uses,
full of Harry's notebooks.

Albums of glossy photos.
The last smile dimmed,
since I heard about Cousin Fanny.

I see the family face
break through the surface
of Grandpa's speckled mirror

and hardly recognise myself.
Every object
claims me as its keeper,

souvenirs of joy
and anger I'm not sure whether
I want to cherish or destroy.

LEARNING ABOUT HIM

A sheep bleated, and sounded
exactly like someone imitating a sheep,
which made me think of my father –

the sort of thing he'd do,
suddenly start to clown and act crazy, or like
a warning cough of static

from the jelly-mould
Art Deco shape of the big valve radio,
its glowing amber dial

marked with places he'd been to.
I'd twiddle the knobs and move the needle through
London, Bombay, Rio.

'Look after my Feigele,'
(the Yiddish name meant little bird) her dying
mother said to the lodger,

my father, so they got married.
I heard the story after his funeral
and finally understood

why I was born in New York.
I'd recognised another melancholic
early on, but not

the auto-didact's hunger
for self-improvement he dissembled (as though
it would be shameful if

any of us knew) until
clearing his room, choosing which books to keep,
I found old favourites.

I hate to read books marked
with comments in the margin, underlinings,
but these were different.

I was learning about him.
For instance, how he'd saved what seemed every
postcard I'd mailed home –

grudgingly dutiful –
and pasted them in scrapbooks, marking my routes
red and his bright blue.

We'd almost meshed the globe.
I wonder if his restlessness was soothed
by mine, or irritated?

Dear father, now your crazy
daughter's weeping sounds like bleating or
a faulty radio.

MY FUCHSIA

My fuchsia is a middle-aged woman
who's had fourteen children, and though
she could do it again, she's rather tired.

All through the summer, new blooms.
I'm amazed. But the purple and crimson
have paled. Some leaves are yellowed or withering.

These buds look weaker and smaller,
like menopause babies. Yet still
she's a gallant fine creature performing her function.

— That's how they talk about women,
and I heard myself using the same sort of language.
Then I understood my love for August:
its exhausted fertility
after glut and harvest.

Out in the garden, playing
at being a peasant forced
to slave until dark with a child on my back

another at the breast and probably
pregnant, I remember
wondering if I'd ever manage

the rites of passage from girl
to woman: fear
and fascination hard to choose between.

Thirty years later, I pick the crumpled flowers
off the fuchsia plant and water it
as if before the shrine
of two unknown grandmothers —
and my mother, who was a fourteenth child.

THE CRESCENT

My stick of lipsalve is worn away
into the same curved crescent
that was the first thing I noticed
about my mother's lipstick.
It marked the pressure of her existence
upon the world of matter.

Imagine the grim fixity
of my stare, watching her smear
the vivid grease across her lips
from a tube shiny as a bullet.
The way she smoothed it
with the tip of a little finger
(the tinge it left, even after
washing her hands, explained
the name 'pinky') and her pointed tongue
licking out like a kitten's,
fascinated, irritated.

It was part of the mystery of
brassières and compacts and handbags
that meant being grown-up. I thought
my own heels would have to grow
a sort of spur to squeeze right down
the narrow hollow inside high-heels.

Now I am calmer and no longer
paint my lips except with this,
pale as a koshered carcass
drained of blood in salty water
or a memorial candle,
wax congealed down one side,
as though it stood in the wind

that blows from the past, flame
reflected like a crescent
moon against a cloud
in the pool of molten light.

I carry the sign of the moon
and my mother, a talisman
in a small plastic tube
in my handbag, a holy relic
melted by believers'
kisses, and every time
I smooth my lips with the unguent
I feel them pout and widen
in the eternal smile
of her survival through me,
feel her mouth on mine.

A DISCUSSION WITH PATRICK KAVANAGH
about his poem: 'Intimate Parnassus'

I could sit here for hours, twisting my rings,
dazed by the light and colour a diamond flashes,
without a thought in my head. An image which must
include everything that went to form me:
the universal gases, ultra violet
infra red, the seams of giant ferns
compressed to carbon. My mother's photo album.

'. . . to be/ Passive, observing with a steady eye',
is the poet's purpose, you wrote, praising
a god-like detachment (another world entirely,
but who would want to argue?) Trying to calm
my frantic heart with such-like axioms
I would guess is not exactly what
you meant, but still the only path I know

apart from total recall: the paraphernalia
of personality – too much baggage
there for transmutation. Staring
in the crystal ball of my mother's diamond ring
doesn't serve to clarify connexions
fused by violent words and acts. The conflict
between poetry and contemplation.

To be passive, observing with a steady eye
(the only duty I acknowledge) needs
a cool ironic style I've not yet managed.
And pondering one's destiny is suspect
from whatever viewpoint, even Parnassus;
forces the language to defensive postures.
My mother's ringless hands keep turning the pages.

LIKE MANET'S 'OLYMPE'

Like Manet's *Olympe*, naked in the afternoon heat
and manilla-shaded light, my aunt lay
on the green watered-silk of her bedspread. Smooth hair,
proud head, short but shapely legs and
high breasts were so much the same as the painting
I had just fallen in love with, that I faltered, still
half in the doorway, almost afraid to enter.

Through one moted beam that cut across the room
between us, I saw her reflection, pale as an ocean
creature, floating deep in the dressing-table mirror
over splinters of sun from the jumble of bottles
and jars – stern eyes seeming to dare me closer.

But this was a small house in Virginia, not
the Paris of artists. In spite of leather-bound volumes
of Schopenhauer and Baudelaire and Saturday
opera broadcasts, her aesthetic was helpless
against suburban power. The loneliness
and vanity and fearfulness which kept her
from dalliance, made me the only possible
audience, and her adoring victim.

About art and beauty, loneliness and
fearfulness and vanity, how much she taught me.

OVID AMONG THE SCYTHIANS
after Delacroix

Marshy banks of the Danube, reeds and bushes
and muddy crescents of horses' hooves. Their
clothes are earth-coloured, his dark blue.

He feels the autumn starting — that sky, those clouds,
the way the wind is moving them. The mountains
roll back, uncharted as far as China.

Ovid is writing another letter to Rome —
a gentle puzzlement to his watchers, which weapons
and dogs don't quite shield them from.

He wonders whether a linen toga, his scrolls
and pens, and their unknowing admiration,
can be protection against such sadness,

if he can metamorphose Chaos to Order,
exile to Fate, the amorous summer weasel
into the noble winter ermine.

DRIVING I

Umber, amber, ochre. Viridian and sepia.
A Victorian painting: *After the Storm*.
The branches seem wrenched by a torturing bully.
Tested and found wanting – a character corroded
by putting money on the wrong horse.
Faster, faster.
The purpose of writing notes
is that the words are not spoken: a system
that would be shattered by articulation.
Sounds heard with the inner ear
surface as slowly
as other disturbances you learn to ignore.
Clay-smeared discs of sawn tree-trunks
like split stones or stained amoebas,
annular pools in the fields like the roots of clouds.
The one who gets blamed always has the power.
Driving is the metaphor.

DRIVING II

Each species is allotted its number of heartbeats.
A mouse has the same life span as myself or a whale
but lives it more quickly, at a different tempo.

The fluttering heat of a heart or a forest.
How many leaves to a kilometre?
I want to be astonished, but it happens less often.

Such solid coils of steam and smoke extruded from
the tall cone-chimneys of a power station,
like chalky turds defying the laws of gravity.

Trees and cars and clouds blur in the speed. I have seen
almost enough for a whole life – endless renewal
and repetition. The planet belongs to the trees.

DRIVING III

Village after village, evidence
filters from the back of the café
louder than the lotto numbers –
people laughing, dogs barking.

A frieze of bright brown chickens
with scarlet combs
that strut and scratch below the hedge,
running interference.

Iron body oozing rust
into the wooden cross,
roadside crucifixes
transubstantiate to brioche.

Behind the garage, a car jacked up
at the inspection pit
like a woman with her legs
in obstetrical stirrups.

The museums of Europe
are textbooks for martyrs.
The river barges inspire noyades.
Two people dragging each other down.

THE DEAD SEA

Nights I don't sleep, however I lie
every limb and organ aches
and though I stretch further up
the pillows, throw the blanket back,
I still can't breathe and the dark vibrates

its molecules into a form
pressing me close from mouth to hip,
stifled under an embrace more
urgent than any human lover's,
when I become his favourite

to float with him upon a sea
of melted bones and curdled clouds
and phosphorescent glass towards
a hidden shore we never reach
through waters where we cannot drown.

THE PLANETARIUM

It makes a difference
whether the earth is at its winter
nearness to, or summer
distance from, the sun.

A few hundred miles change climate
and terrain from ice
to jungle, north to south,
every fact of life.

Which seems strange, compared
to the vastnesses of space
(my first visit
to the Planetarium

fixed an image of blackness
struggling against
a fragile net of light)
yet comforting, because

a millimetre's alteration
in the angle at
the corner of your mouth
can have the same importance.

STRING

Unknotting the string you tied
my fingers make the same movements
but in the opposite order
undoing what you did

while smoothness sheathes my skin
with its electric aura
as if our hands entangled
space and time

and the rough twine recalls
your morning face,
tales of knots impossible
to loose – how they were untied.

SISTER, SISTER

Sister, sister, I am sick.
Come and give me meat and drink.
Let me eat from your hand.

    *   *   *

Amnon lay on his bed, moaning
with lust and vexation, knowing
that Tamar was still a virgin

by the special colour of her dress.
(Such was the custom for a princess.)
'Come closer, sister, you

yourself shall be my meat and drink.'
He ran his tongue around her wrist.
She could not make him stop.

'The sweetest food is your hair and flesh.'
First he wheedled, then he threatened.
She argued, 'Do not force me.'

Those words meant less to him than the insects'
drone outside the curtained window
or incense fumes trapped

between the roofbeams, and he was stronger.
Afterwards, he could no longer
bear that tragic face,

called a slave to bolt the door
and keep the woman out. She tore
the bodice of her dress

(lost, the right to wear it now)
daubed with ashes head and brow,
hurt more by his hatred

than her ravishment. What
did Tamar think when Absalom,
two years later, killed him?

The story leaves her desolate,
but doesn't tell. One has to guess.
I imagine Tamar

in her chamber, burning incense
and remembering. The insects'
whining seems a song:

'Sister, sister, I am sick.
Come and give me meat and drink.
Let me eat from your hand.'

CUP AND SWORD

The cup has to be stone,
cup-holes
in the lower face of the protecting boulder
dripping stone-milk.

Which means that the sword
is Excalibur –
King Arthur's slashing sword –
hard-belly, the voracious one.

Those bodies in bloody armour
were knights-errant
who fought to hold their cavern,
keep the cup hidden.

Something that started a long time ago
can still nourish –
like a Grail story –
though the cup is empty, the sword broken.

THE RESTLESSNESS OF SUNSET

I pull the curtains to
open them again
get up from my desk
sit down stand up again

to go to the window
and watch the changes
of cloud and colour
every moment changing

and every afternoon
as dusk begins
I can't stay still
or close myself in

until the sun has gone
behind the trees below the line
of the horizon
until the sky

has dulled and darkened
enough to let
the evening start
and soothe the restlessness of sunset.

THE SAME POWER

Lush chill of spring in Holland Park.
Dark glassy flesh of the bluebells, hoarse
cry of a peacock strutting his courtship cope
against a wind which flattens it out behind
and ripples the quills like waves on a squally sea.
Striated bark of birch trees' pale trunks
as sharp a white as opening hawthorn flowers.
Vivid rainclouds scudding across the sky.

Which all must be attended to now,
not half-ignored, only recalled later (perhaps) –
that common regret for not having been alert
enough to recognise the one moment
when beauty, truth, life and death became
the same Power: evoked not described.

THAT PRESENCE

Like a painter stepping backward from the easel,
straightening up from the worktable,
with a loaded brush, to see exactly where
another touch of red is wanted, like
a carpet weaver wondering if the time
has come to change the pattern, a sculptor
hesitating before the first decisive cut,
I ponder a poem, repeating every word,
trying to hear where a note needs altering,
testing by breath and sense and luck,

like staring at the surface of a mirror
through soundless levels between glass and silver
into the pupils of that reflected presence
over my shoulder advancing from its depths.

IN DRUMMOND'S ROOM
(*William Drummond of Hawthornden,*
1585–1649)

This morning, after
lighting the fire, I looked
from the deep window of Drummond's room

over the glen
toward clouds so dark that the black
horizon-trees blurred against them.

Only the flames were bright,
burning under the pilgrims'
scallop-shells carved on the mantel.

Then the wind veered,
the wood smoked, and the tall yew
whose needled boughs

fill the other window
soughed, louder than
the logs' seething, and through the glass

splinters of colour—
the red excited push
of growth, the yellow of last year's leaves

that strengthens green,
patches of blue, sun and shadow—
signalled a new front

of weather moving in.
For an hour or two at noon
the sky was clear. But I prefer

to stay in here
and build the fire up, squeeze
the bellows, watch exactly how

sparks jump and
the cinders shimmer, how
the branches turn and lift at the same

agitated angle
as the sudden-falling slant
of whirling snow that will not settle

and the calm curve
of the sunset rainbow
above the swollen river,

to disentangle
the single pattern through each
recurrence and renewal since

he stared into the fire
and from the windows, to see
and feel and think what I do now.

THE WITTERSHAM SIBYL

The pattern of dew on spiders' webs
and how it hung like crystal beads,
every hole the birds had torn —
pucker-edged and starfish-shaped
for frost and rain to work upon —
through fallen apples lacquer-bright
among the swathes of dripping fern,

these, and the angles the rising wind
bent from the pampas' papery leaves
and straw-pale peeling stems, the way
the shattered-topaz acorn husks
livid toadstools and rusty moss
reclaimed the lawn, she knew must be
messages from the god.

THE NOVELTY

Winter's charcoal structures and autumn's flaring challenge
after summer fattens spring's sketchy foliage:
like a million gas-jets,
crocuses ignite beneath the warming boughs.

Meadows flushing green for what seems just a day
before their tawny paleness is stacked away as harvest,
ponds sink low and hedges wither.
Lambs becoming sheep, and babies, parents.

Then months of frost and clouded skies until the change
from open fires to windows; and as the sun approaches
the extreme of solstice,
the novelty of watching it all start again.

THE POET –

    sits at her desk, watching an insect
moving its antennae in time
with Mozart. A quiet evening in August,

invoking the melancholy pleasure
of aimless thought. Knowing that what
goes unrecorded is written on water.
The ripples disperse, as is their nature.

But beyond the roofs, the crescent
moon and stars seem points and markers
of a limitless expansion.

Later, she might wonder whether
something precious was squandered, ointments
poured extravagantly out
(almost swooning from the odours).

The torment starts whose cure is nothing less
than pen and ink and paper –
    and the entire universe.

Translations

Translations of poems
from the Portuguese
by Sophia de Mello Breyner

Sophia de Mello Breyner was born in 1919 at Oporto in northern Portugal. She studied Classics at Lisbon University, and was already a recognised poet by the mid 1940's. She became a Deputy in the Constituent Assembly after the overthrow of the Salazar regime, and was President of the Portuguese Writers' Association. As well as poetry, she has published collections of children's stories, critical essays, and translations of Shakespeare and Dante. She has received numerous prizes for her work.

MID-DAY

Mid-day. No one in this corner of the beach.
The sun on high, deep, enormous, open
Has cleared the sky of every god.
Implacable as punishment, light falls.
There are no ghosts, nor souls,
And the huge, solitary, ancient ocean
Seems to applaud.

from: Poesia (Poetry), 1944

ONE DAY

One day dead tired worn out we shall
Go back and live as plainly as animals
Even so tired again we shall flourish
Living brothers of the sea and the pinewoods.

The wind will blow away our weariness
The thousand unreal anxious gestures
And our slack limbs surely will regain
The weightless speed of animals.

Only then shall we be able to move
Through the mystery nurtured and lulled
By green pinewoods and the sea's voice
And let its words grow in us.

from: Dio do Mar (Day of the Sea), 1947

DAY OF THE SEA

Day of sea in the sky, made
From shadows and horses and plumes.

Day of sea in my room — cube
Where my sleepwalker's movements slide
Between animal and flower, like medusas.

Day of sea in the sky, high day
Where my gestures are seagulls who lose themselves
Spiralling over the clouds, over the spume.

from: Coral (Coral), 1950

SIBYLS

Sibyls of deep caves, of petrefaction.
Totally loveless and sightless,
Feeding nothingness as if a sacred fire
While shadow unmakes night and day
Into the same light of fleshless panic.

Drive out that foul dew
Of impacted nights, the sweat
Of forces turned against themselves
When words batter the walls
In blind, wild swoops of trapped birds
And the horror of being winged
Shrills like a clock through a vacuum.

from: Coral, 1950

LISTEN

Listen:
Everything is calm and smooth and sleeping.
The walls apparent, the floor reflecting,
And painted on the glass of the window,
The sky, green emptiness, two trees.
Close your eyes and rest no less profoundly
Than any other thing which never flowered.

Don't touch anything, don't look, don't recollect.
One step enough
To shatter the furniture baked
By endless, unused days of sunlight.

Don't remember, don't anticipate.
You do not share the nature of a fruit.
Nothing here that time or sun will ripen.

from: Coral, 1950

BEACH

The pines moan when the wind passes
The sun beats on the earth and the stones burn.

Fantastic sea gods stroll at the edge of the world
Crusted with salt and brilliant as fishes.

Sudden wild birds hurled
Against the light into the sky like stones
Mount and die vertically
Their bodies taken by space.

The waves butt as if to smash the light
Their brows ornate with columns.

And an ancient nostalgia of being a mast
Sways in the pines.

from: Coral, 1950

TORPID SHORES

Torpid shores open their arms,
And a great ship departs in silence.
Gulls fly at high perpendicular angles,
The light is born, and death is perfect.

A great ship departs, abandoning
The white columns of a vacant harbour.
And its own face seeks itself emerging
From the headless torso of the city.

A great ship unloosed departs
Sculpting head-on the north wind.
Perfect the ocean's blue, death perfect —
Awesome clear sharp forms.

from: Coral, 1950

IN THE POEM

To bring the picture the wall the wind
The flower the glass the shine on wood
And the cold clear chasteness of water
To the clean severe world of the poem

To save from death decay and ruin
The actual moment of vision and surprise
And keep in the real world
The real gesture of a hand touching the table.

from: Livro Sexto (Sixth Book), 1962

MUSE

Muse teach me the song
Revered and primordial
The song for everyone
Believed by all

Muse teach me the song
The true brother of each thing
Incendiary of the night
And evening's secret

Muse teach me the song
That takes me home
Without delay or haste
Changed to plant or stone

Or changed into the wall
Of the first house
Or become the murmur
Of sea all around

(I remember the floor
Of well-scrubbed planks
Its soapy smell
Keeps coming back)

Muse teach me the song
Of the sea's breath
Heaving with brilliants
Muse teach me the song
Of the white room
And the square window

So I can say
How evening there
Touched door and table
Cup and mirror
How it embraced

Because time pierces
Time divides
And time thwarts
Tears me alive
From the walls and floor
Of the first house

Muse teach me the song
Revered and primordial
To fix the brilliance
Of the polished morning

That rested its fingers
Gently on the dunes
And whitewashed the walls
Of those simple rooms

Muse teach me the song
That chokes my throat

from: Livro Sexto (Sixth Book), 1962

TWILIGHT OF THE GODS

A smile of amazement appeared in the Aegean islands
And Homer made royal-purple flower on the sea
The Kouros moved forward exactly one step
Athena's paleness glittered in the daylight

In that time the gods' clarity conquered the monsters
                    on all the temple pediments
And the Persians retreated to their empire's furthest limits.

We celebrated the victory: darkness
Was exposed and sacrificed in great white courtyards
The hoarse cry of the chorus purified the city

Swift joy circled the ships
Like dolphins
Our body was naked because it had found
Its exact measure
We invented: the light inherent to Sounion's columns
Each day the world became more ours

But then they were extinguished
The ancient gods, internal sun of things
Then there opened the void which separates us from things
We are hallucinated by absence, drunk with absence
And to Julian's heralds, the Sibyl replied:

'Go tell the king that the beautiful palace lies broken
                    on the ground
Phoebus now has no house nor prophetic bay-tree nor
                    melodious fountain
The talking water is silent'

from: Geografia (Geography), 1967

303

THE SMALL SQUARE

My life had taken the form of a small square
That autumn when your death was being meticulously
organised
I clung to the square because you loved
The humble and nostalgic humanity of small shops
Where shopkeepers fold and unfold ribbons and cloth
I tried to become you because you were going to die
And all my life there would cease to be mine
I tried to smile as you smiled
At the newspaper seller at the tobacco seller
At the woman without legs who sold violets
I asked the woman without legs to pray for you
I lit candles at all the altars
Of the churches standing in the corners of that square
Hardly had I opened my eyes when I saw and read
The vocation for eternity written on your face
I summoned up the streets places people
Who were the witnesses of your face
So they would call you so they would unweave
The tissue that death was binding around you

from: Duál (Dual), 1972

CYCLADES
(*invoking Fernando Pessoa*)

The frontal clarity of this place imposes your presence
Your name emerges as if the negative
Of what you were develops here

You lived in reverse
Incessant traveller of the inverse
Exempt from yourself
Widower of yourself
Lisbon your stage-set
You were the tenant of a rented room above a dairy
Competent clerk in a business firm
Ironic delicate polite frequenter of the Old Town bars
Judicious visionary of cafés facing the Tagus

(Where still in the marble-topped tables
We seek the cold trace of your hands
– Their imperceptible fingering)

Dismembered by the furies of that non-life
Marginal to yourself to others and to life
You kept all your notebooks up to date
With meticulous exactitude drew the maps
Of the multiple navigations of your absence –

What never was and what you never were stays said
Like an island rising up windward
With plumb-line compass astrolabe and sounding-lead
You determined the measure of exile

You were born later
Others had found the truth
The sea-route to India already was discovered

305

Nothing was left of the gods
But their uncertain passage
Through the murmur and smell of those landscapes
And you had many faces
So that being no-one you could say everything
You travelled the reverse the inverse the adverse

And yet obstinately I invoke – O divided one –
The instant that might unite you
And celebrate your arrival at the islands you never reached

These are the archipelagos that float across your face
The swift dolphins of joy
The gods did not grant nor you wanted

This is the place where the flesh of statues like trembling
willows
Pierced by light's breathing
Shines with matter's blue breath
On beaches where mirrors turn towards the sea

Here the enigma that always puzzled me
Is more naked and vehement therefore I implore:

'Why were your movements broken
Who encircled you by walls and chasms
Who spilt your secrets onto the ground'

Invoke you as though you arrived in this boat
And it were your feet stepping onto the islands
Whose excessive overwhelming nearness
Was like a loved face bending too close

In the summer of this place I call you
Who hibernated your life like an animal through the harsh
season

Who needed to be distant like someone standing back to see
                                                    the picture better
And willed the distance he suffered

I call you — I gather the pieces the ruins the fragments —
Because the world cracked like a quarry
And capitals and arms columns shattered to splinters
Heave from the ground
And only a scattering of potsherds is left of the amphora
Before which the gods become foreigners

Yet here the wheat-coloured goddesses
Raise the long harp of their fingers
To charm the blue sun where I invoke you
And invoke the impersonal word of your absence

If only this festive moment could break your mourning
O self-elected widower
And if being and to be would coincide
In the one marriage

As if your boat were waiting in Thasos
As if Penelope
In her high chamber
Were weaving you into her hair

from: O Nome das Coisas (In the Name of Things), 1977

307

THE ISLANDS

I

We navigated East –
The long coast
Was a dense somnolent green

A motionless green under an absent wind
As far as the white shore colour of roses
Touched by transparent waters

Then appeared the luminous islands
Of a blue so pure and violent
Surpassing the brilliance of heavens
Navigated by miraculous herons

And memory and time were quenched

II

Abstract navigation
Intent as a fish the plane follows the route
Seen from above the earth becomes a map

But suddenly
We cross into the Orient through the great gate
Of blue sapphires in the glinting sea

III

The light of dawn's appearance
Shone in the hollow of wandering
Sails testing the distances

Here they let down the dark anchors
Those who went seeking
The real face of the visible
And dared – most fantastic adventure –
To live the whole of the possible

IV

> Dolce color d'oriental zaffiro
> Dante – *Purgatorio, Canto I*

Here they sighted islands rise like flowers
Those who came by sea heading south
And rounded the cape to face the dawn sky
Steering the thrust of the black keels

And under tall clouds like white lyres
Their eyes truly saw
The sweet blue of the East and of sapphires

V

We saw the visible in all its vehemence
The total exposure of appearance
And what we had not dared to dream
Was real

VI

They navigated from the chart they had to make

(Leaving behind the plots and conversations
Muffled intrigues of brothel and palace)

The wise men had already concluded
That only the known could exist:
Ahead lay only the unnavigable
Below the sun's clamour, the uninhabitable

Undeciphered the writing of those other stars
In the silence of cloudy zones
The shivering compass needle touching space

Then appeared the luminous coasts
Silences the palm-groves' ardent coolness
And the brilliance of the visible face to face

VII

Difficult to face your death head-on
And never expect you again in the mirrors of fog

from: Navigacoes (Navigations), 1983

WRITING

In Palazzo Mocenigo where he lived alone
Lord Byron used every grand room
To watch solitude mirror by mirror
And the beauty of doors no one passed through

He heard the marine murmurs of silence
The lost echoes of steps in far corridors
He loved the smooth shine on polished floors
Shadows unrolling under high ceilings
And though he sat in just one chair
Was glad to see the other chairs were empty

Of course no one needs so much space to live
But writing insists on solitudes and deserts
Things to look at as if seeing something else

We can imagine him seated at his table
Imagine the full long throat
The open white shirt
The white paper the spidery writing
And the light of a candle – as in certain paintings –
Focussing all attention

from: Ilhas (Islands), 1990

Translations of poems
from the French
by Jean Joubert

Jean Joubert was born in 1928 in Châlette-sur-Loing (Loiret), France. He has lived in Languedoc for the last 25 years and was Professor of American Literature at the Université Paul Valéry at Montpellier. He has published novels and children's stories as well as poetry. His collection *Poèmes: 1955–1975* (Grasset, 1975) was awarded the prize of the Académie Mallarmé in 1978.

THE LETTER

Tonight you were ten thousand years old
you were the mountain with nine doors
with its forests gorges and peaks
its boulders its thickets
bare branches meshes of foliage
its tears smiles mosses ferns
its spoor of lightning deer and ants

Tonight you were a thousand years old
a millenium of mills and vines
taverns and high walls
orchards sheep tracks and churches

You were twenty tonight
Tonight you were the same age as the poem
because a sorceress said I was immortal
and because you are in the poem
like the fruit in the flower
and the seed in the fruit

Oh Ronsard, bearded old fogey
with a garland of box a quill behind your ear
runny nose and gouty foot
shaking the rattles of time and eternity
to dazzle some beauty 'in the green of her age'
hoary old poet searching the inkwell
for the final weapon the final tear
as from this place of mist and dream
I do the same for you tonight

THE TWO SISTERS

At the edge of the black water
lived the sisters,
those two confederates of the fog.

In their floating window,
each evening burned the mystery of lamps.
Wings and vapours seethed above the marsh.

We children believed this was cursed ground,
a blend of fire and water, and we fled
hopping through the village.

On the Day of the Dead, they opened their door
and we went to fetch the funeral wreaths,
our faces clenched against the bitter smell of box.

IS IT THE WIND?

Is it the wind that rules us?
This one, crossing the marsh,
ferrying dreams and crimes?
Or that proud friend of the snow
where the soul slides and floats on the peaks?
Or is it yet another —
outburst of anger, gasp of shadow,
metamorphosis, at dawn, of the forest
where watery leaves tremble?

As the orchard emerges, each morning
    I ask myself these questions.

I feel them shake, the reins that link me
to countless invisible stars, the just-set moon
and sunlight splashing colour
on the hill. Through every tree
and flower, through the veins of the garden,
sap flows. It drenches my palms.
A dog walks across my gaze.
The cat yawns near a rose, while
further off magpies rustle the branches.
And the young light intensifies the form
of a web where the archangel watches.
Together we pray. In silence we receive
and accept this great breath that laves us.

PORTRAIT OF THE ARTIST

Seated, small, legs crossed, this
speck, this almost nothing, is a
man who smokes, thinks
writes. The sand is dark;
mica, striated eroded stone.
In the stream, from fall to fall,
trout leap; dwarf willow
sway their fleecy manes;
shadows scorch the slopes
where sheep peal.
On the peaks messengers
breathe mysteries and marvels,
and invisible stars, the beautiful dead,
sail through blue infinity.
Close your eyes, turn from the mirror
and in your own night most humbly measure
joy – the gift of vertigo.

SITTING BY THE WINDOW

Sitting by the window, a little girl spells out
words from a heavy book on her knees.
Eyes fixed, her temples are hidden by
disordered dark hair, and the flowered pink skirt
rides up over bare thighs where
light that filters through the leaves plays.
Now and then the mouth breathes a bubble:
'The child slipped into the mirror . . .'
'The thunder prowls . . .' 'Do you love me?'
words mumbled as if by heart.
A fly buzzes through the silence afterwards,
and in the kitchen's shadows
an old woman shifts cloths and knives.
Against the cream plastered walls
flares the blood of a geranium,
while the butcher (apron, beret, moustache)
passes, bent double, a headless carcass
across his shoulders. It's almost
noon, in Beauce, summer, in a flat village
where the wind drags the dull smell of wheat.

MIDI

The smell that rises from kitchens must please the gods
and the stewpot has the same value as the poem's alembic
where metaphors seethe. Also I say:
prayer, thanksgiving, offering; and regret
forgetting to serve the invisible ones,
those effigies of clay on their simple altar.
Let these fumes at least be the homage
heavenly nostrils enjoy, likewise distant, likewise
lost on the peaks of our misty metaphysics.
Close to the ovens men and gods finally reconcile
the split between flesh and spirit. To that lair
belongs the half-light of sanctuaries, the faithful hand,
the murmur and the low flame where greases fume.
Copper serves as well as gold, parsley as incense;
the geranium against the window turns it into stained glass
where just enough red and green light sifts through.
(The white laboratories, clenched by ice,
only release the works of death, a limbo
of simulacrums, broths for young robots.)
Here herbs, garlic, and onions hang from the beams
and the path to the garden is well trodden,
like those ancient routes where caravans of spices
jangled and swayed. It's right that women reign here,
with their taste for heaven and earth mixed,
and that the heart commits itself to metamorphosis.
(Nevertheless, the kitchens empty like convents
when men probe the mysteries. Ah, bearded poet,
I love your cabbage soup as much as your verse!)
Then later, around the table, the modest dead
will seat themselves among us, and we
shall barely hear their napkins unfold in the shadows.

BIRTHPLACE

That wind which all at once rises in the night
like a hurt voice, like the breath
of those who have crossed the threshold,
loosed the thread, were suddenly swept
into a formless space, into a heavy rain of ash
where the last glimmers
of a stifled fire prowl and founder,

that wind which one would say
meant snow on the tulips,
which brought the April lilacs
to their knees in the garden —
assails the house, sucks at the empty rooms
wants to speak from a thousand blurred mouths
wants to breathe the nearness of the secret
to the one inclined towards it —
unexpectedly permeable, bodiless.

Empty chair, lowered curtain, dust-curls
and the staircase where an old smell lingers.
A ghostly hand brushes the banisters,
hesitates and fades away.
A hair on the floor startles the ants,
and the coat hanging behind the door
mimes the absent one, the half-made gesture.

But with dawn, the wind drops, licks the earth,
nuzzles and probes it,
then spits out seeds and pollens
and, within the sweet odour of death,
exhales the promise of a child.

WOODEN BRIDGE OVER DRAC TORRENT

Once the wind has passed
what are we,
which echo of our dreams?

The sound of steps
on the planks,
grey water breathing a shadow,

while over the forest
a bird lets fly
its last call.

And then such silence
such clearness grind us
into this space without space

where silence and clearness
fuse and dissolve
into indescribable cold.

What are we, lost
beyond limits or memory –
transparent, immobile?

while somewhere else
water slides between arches
and the bird blindly
follows its flight.

THREE WHITE HORSES

Three white horses under my window
grazing the field of the dead
where brushwood chokes the olives.

She said: 'In the night, I saw
your black cat on the roof-ridge,
against the moon.'
She crossed her fingers for luck,
burned tapers, scented death,
read the saints and the sorcerers
to soothe her insomnia.

She said, pressing fists against her belly,
'There's a fire here, that burns me.'

She died during a bright December,
and was carried to the cypress on the hill
where the gravestone she'd chosen waited.

Under my window, she had a poplar planted
for its leaves, its murmur,

which also was burned by the fire,
and died.

The horses graze between the thistles,
neighing, showing their teeth,
ruffling their manes.

In the night, I hear them
down by the wall,

dreaming and breathing
nearby,
as if we shared the same bed,
our bodies confused,
our eyes fixed on ghosts and stars.

DIOGENES

Diogenes, in his tub, pats his dog
that yawns and scratches itself.
'Let's love each other, and share everything!
Whatever's good for you suits me.
Your eye can teach me more wisdom
than Plato, who says I'm crazy,
but frets himself with Ideas and riches,
talks of fire and lives in ashes.
This world is our business.
We don't need much, and afterwards,
we turn to contemplate our kingdom:
earth, sun, wind
and the sea where soon I'll swim naked.
Skin and hair are enough to wear,
bread, figs and bones to fill our bellies.
Yet, come noon, I'll light my lamp
and search through the streets for *a man*
without much hope, in this vile town.
Sometimes I dream that the gods will send
a young and handsome disciple
to share my nights and hard bed.'

AT THE ASSEMBLY

'I demand,' he said, 'the abolition of death'.

Silence in the hall, then a murmur.

'The citizen-representative must have made a mistake,' said
        President Duplessis-Latour. 'Would he care to
        reformulate . . .'

But the other, standing upright, repeated the same words.

'Madman!' shouted the President. 'I call upon you, in the name
        of the Republic, to withdraw your proposal.'

'I maintain it,' he repeated in a firm voice. 'I have nothing else
        to ask here.'

Guards were called, who seized him without the least
        resistance.

In the ambulance taking him across town, he sobbed for a
        long time.

THE WORDS

Autumn came early that year, and the sun was low, the earth grey and the moon pale, swathed in mists. Joseph felt the weight of age on his shoulders, not like a laughing child who wanted to be carried to the spring, but like the dark hide of an animal. He looked at the moon, the earth and the sun as he had done every other day, receiving their strength and light, but his eyes were weaker and his vision confused, he half-closed the lids and thought he could see great curved shadows marching along the roads of the sky.

Already in September the leaves began to fall: yellow leaves from the birch, red leaves from the maple, brown leaves from the beech. And in the garden, petals from the last roses.

The birds set off towards the south, and Joseph heard their plaintive cries until they were far out over the sea.

And then it was words that began to leave him. At first the names of friends who had died, for which he searched his memory in vain. Then the name of the village his family came from. Of a woman he had loved. One morning, he picked an object from the table, and that object no longer had a name. Little by little, other words went like the leaves and the birds over the sea. Things were still there, he could see them, touch them, breathe them, but he did not know what to call them and before long he gave up, while a world of silence thickened inside him. He still clung to some certitudes: 'This is a table, bread, wine, a knife. Yes, but that? And that?' Would he come to forget his own name?

He no longer saw anyone, and only spoke in order to retain, to caress, these last words like familiar animals whose presence comforts in solitude. One after another they became doughy, shapeless, they melted like wax before the fire.

Soon snow began to fall upon the flat fields and, for some days, he could still name it: snow.

Libretti

THE DANCER HOTOKE

libretto for a chamber opera written with the composer
Erika Fox
for the Royal Opera House's 1991 *Garden Venture*,
and nominated for the Laurence Olivier Awards 1992
in category:
Outstanding achievement in opera.

Kiyomori, the great war lord, is persuaded by Gio, his
favourite, to watch a performance by the famous dancer
Hotoke. He is smitten by her grace and beauty and dismisses
Gio, who goes with her mother to a distant retreat where they
both become nuns. Hotoke is remorseful and, unable to accept
the situation, joins Gio in a life of prayer and contemplation.

Characters: 3 singers, puppeteer and puppet

Travelling PRIEST	baritone
KIYOMORI, a war lord	
HOTOKE	soprano and puppet
GIO	mezzo-soprano
Gio's MOTHER	non-singing part taken by puppeteer

Scene I Priest, Hotoke, Gio, Gio's Mother.

THREE WOMEN: *kneeling in place as the lights rise*
Buddha's incarnation
is earth, water, wind, fire, space —
the same five elements
from which we all are made.

PRIEST: *enters. He repeats their prayer.*
Buddha's incarnation
is earth, water, wind, fire, space —
the same five elements
from which we all are made.
You pious women —
why are you here
in this lonely place?

HOTOKE: *rising and coming toward him*
We are nuns
praying for our souls
and every soul on earth.
She is Gio,
who was the mistress of a great war lord,
and this is her aged mother.
I am Hotoke. I was a dancer.
Let me tell you our story.

Gio and Hotoke remove their nuns' robes, revealing rich kimonos. Priest puts on the costume of a war lord.

   Scene II Kiyomori, seated, smoking a long pipe.
      Gio, Hotoke (singer and puppet)

GIO: *approaching*
My lord, they say that Hotoke,
the famous dancer,
is here in the camp.

KIYOMORI:
    I do not care for dancing.
    Send her away.

GIO:
    They say she is as beautiful
    as a reed that sways in the stream
    or the bending crown
    of a tree in the wind —
    the incarnation of dance.
    And she has come so far.
    Let us see her once.

KIYOMORI:
    To please you,
    I will let her dance for us.

HOTOKE:
    Thank you, Gio
    You are as kind as a sister.

She bows to Kiyomori, then steps to one side, and from behind her, the puppeteer appears and manipulates the puppet, dressed in the same costume as Hotoke.

KIYOMORI: *overcome with admiration*
    A reed that sways in the stream,
    a tree that bends in the wind,
    like the incarnation of dance.

GIO:
    I am so happy that my lord is pleased —

KIYOMORI: *ignoring her*
    Come, Hotoke.
    he pats the matting next to him
    Sit here by my side.

HOTOKE: *hesitant*
    But that is the place of the favourite.

333

KIYOMORI:
    Now you are my favourite.
    In you I shall embrace
    the spirit of dance made flesh.

GIO: *hurt and dignified*
    I brought her to this,
    and brought this on myself.
    Favour is fleeting
    as foam on a breaking wave.
    I must accept my fate
    and take the stony road
    to the wilderness,
    to the wind-swept emptiness,
    to be a nun
    for the rest of my days.

She moves upstage, where she silently puts on her nun's robe and then slowly crosses from one side to the other during the next scene.

Scene III Kiyomori, Hotoke (singer and puppet)

KIYOMORI:
    Now you are my favourite.
    I shall give you costly robes and jewels,
    painted scrolls and fans,
    pools of golden carp.

HOTOKE: *following her own line of thought*
    I wonder how Gio fares
    on the stony road
    to the wilderness?

KIYOMORI:
    You are so beautiful –

HOTOKE:
    Gio was more beautiful.

KIYOMORI:
    Forget her.

HOTOKE:
    She was as kind as a sister.
    Yet we have both come to this.
    I feel remorse to be
    the cause of her banishment.

KIYOMORI: *attempting to embrace her*
    In you I embrace
    the spirit of dance
    that burns like a flame
    through the clear glass
    of a closed lamp,
    not a woman of flesh.

The puppet dancer reappears. Kiyomori tries to embrace it, but it eludes him.

HOTOKE:
    You only know the one who dances.
    You only see the dancer,
    not the one who is remorseful.
She puts on the nun's robe and moves upstage.
    I follow the stony road
    to the place where she is.
    I shall be a nun
    and spend the rest of my days
    in the wilderness
    with Gio and her mother.

Kiyomori moves upstage other side, where he removes the war lord trappings, reverting to character of Priest

    Scene IV Hotoke, Gio, Gio's Mother, Priest.

HOTOKE: *She appears weary and travel-stained, as if after many days on the road, and delighted to find Gio and her mother.*

I have followed your road
through wind and rain and snow,
climbed high mountains,
forded wide rivers
and crossed the deep waters.

GIO:
    You have come like a sister —

HOTOKE:
    It always was our fate
    to be here together —

GIO & MOTHER:
    — for the rest of our days
    to pray for every soul on earth
    and the soul of each other.

PRIEST:
    How strange it is,
    the story of Gio and Hotoke,
    always together
    in this lonely place
    in the wilderness
    of the elements
    earth
    water
    wind
    fire
    space

THE EUROPEAN STORY

libretto for a chamber opera written with the composer
Geoffrey Alvarez
for the Royal Opera House's 1993 *Garden Venture*
(based on the poem, *The European Story*, from *The Knot*,
1990)

A woman writer makes contact with archetypes of her own and
of 'European' consciousness, and experiences a *rite de pasage*
which involves integrating them into the totality of her being.

Characters:

JUDITH – lyric soprano
A young woman writer.

CHORUS – dramatic soprano
Her rational, organising, contemporary intellect.

CRONE – contralto
A Sibylline, ancient Wise Woman, her 'collective
subconscious'. Wears dark robe and headcovering.

MAN – bass baritone
A personification of everything masculine, positive and
negative. The threatening and aggressive, but also active
and constructive parts of her nature. He is dressed in
medieval doublet & hose.

The Crone and Man are 'archetypal figures', and therefore assume different identities during the course of the piece. Chorus is also a projection of Judith's psyche: the explicator and interpreter who, as in Elizabethan drama, comments upon the course of events. She alone does not mutate into different identities, which are:

JUDITH: sacrificial daughter, veiled woman, puppet-killer, Joan, girl-soldier/Crusader

CRONE: cave-crone, Judith's 'Stone-Age self', rooting goddess

MAN: puppet, soldier on the run, antlered masker, Angel, Old Man of the Sea, surgeon

The action occurs in the timelessness of Judith's mental world, and in her present-day study, where the piece is set.

Scene I

Judith, seated at her desk, writing.
Chorus, looking over Judith's shoulder at her work.

JUDITH:
    A story?
    There's not enough action –

CHORUS:
    Just an endless loping
    through the cobwebbed aisles and arches
    of a Gothic forest –

JUDITH:
    – unreeling like a painted backcloth.

CHORUS: *agreeing*
    Not enough action.

JUDITH: *decisively*
    Unless it is
    to break the mould.

The Man runs in, holding out his hand with a large red heart
resting on the palm.

CHORUS, JUDITH:
They turn towards him, shocked. They divide the
following lines between them.
    Red cheeked.
    Raw boned.
    Black mustachioed.
    A puppet escaped from its master,
    a soldier on the run.

MAN:
    I did the murder,
    cut her open.

CHORUS:
    Then he stumbles –

MAN: *stumbling*
   — and the heart in the cup of my bloodied palm
   bounces into the ferns.
Throws Heart to Judith, who catches it.

CRONE: *approaches Man, touches his hand and releases him.*
   My son, my son, have you hurt yourself?
   My dear, don't fall!

Scene II

JUDITH: *moving away from her desk*
   My mother might have told that story.
   Cave-crone guarding the fire spark
   as safe inside its ball of clay and moss
   as an infant lapped by womb water,
   she handed on the ancient curse —

CRONE:
   — ancient curse, ancient curse —

CHORUS:
   The lesson you refused to learn —

CRONE: *caressing the heart*
   Mother-tongue mumbling heart words.

This phrase repeated, fragmented, behind Chorus's next lines.

CHORUS:
   A test, a test,
   the story is a test
   to prove Death weaker than mother-love,
   and reconcile the sacrificial daughters.

CRONE:
   My dear, don't fall!

Scene III

JUDITH:
   — break the mould — break the mould —

340

CHORUS: *explanatory*
>   She has been formed by what the story means.
>   Her first cry was a protest.

JUDITH:
Her tone that of someone learning truths about herself:
surprised and overwhelmed.
>   I was born in a smothering caul,
>   a veiled woman.
>   I feared –

MAN: *picks up antlered mask and sings through its mouth:*
>   – the antlered maskers' shadow,

JUDITH:
>   I feared –

MAN:
>   – the Wild Hunt's shout and echo,

JUDITH:
>   I feared –

CRONE: *puts on necklace of dead piglets*
>   – the rooting goddess who eats her farrow.

Music to take Judith from fear to swagger.

JUDITH: *swaggering*
>   In dreams –
>   In dreams –
>   In dreams I was the puppet-killer,
>   her defender,

Man & Judith in collusion, as if dancing during next
exchanges.

Crone offers Judith sword and breastplate.

MAN:
>   with sword and dagger sharper than the Angel's,
>   armour –

JUDITH: *striking 'Joan of Arc' pose*
    – brighter than Joan's.

CHORUS: *to Judith*
    But could not find the right disguise to fool her,
    neither child nor mother with your child.

JUDITH: *throwing off armour*
    Oh what grief, never to hear
    that special note in her voice –

CRONE:
    My son, my son, have you hurt yourself?

JUDITH: *gesturing with sword*
    You want to plunge the knife
    into your own heart.

Scene IV

CHORUS: *to Judith*
    Cast your bread on the waters.

MAN: *draping seaweed – or something 'marine' – over his head*
    But the Old Man of the Sea
    rises up and straddles your shoulders.

CHORUS:
    He's wet and cold and heavy.

JUDITH: *more emotional*
    Wet/Cold/Heavy

CHORUS:
    You stagger and almost drown.

JUDITH: *staggering*
    Then up from the ground between your feet

MAN: *viciously*
  another one comes
  and splits you open,
  thrusts his hand in the shambles

JUDITH:
  wrenches out your heart.

JUDITH AND CRONE:
  When he stumbles and drops it
  the heart cries out:
  My dear, don't fall!

*Judith sings 'My dear . . .' in exactly the same tone as Crone
– which fuels her angry energy in the next scene.*

Scene V

JUDITH: *desperate and determined*
  Change the heart into a ticking bomb –

MAN: *handing her a large black bomb*
  – the soldier to a girl,
  the very last Crusader –

JUDITH:
  Sure that a dark Annunciation chose her
  to throw that bomb,
  and break the whole world's heart.

CRONE:
  Don't hurt my heart!
This is like a conditioned reflex to the word 'heart'.

JUDITH, MAN:*gleefully, linked and swaying like drunks*
  That moves the story on!

CHORUS:
  A test, a test,
  the story is a test,
  and if you pass the test –

343

CRONE: *still the tone of a conditioned reflex*
My dear, don't fall!

CHROUS: *leading the chorus of the other 2, 'setting the agenda'*
Her ideas and actions

JUDITH:
My ideas and actions

CRONE:
– ideas and actions –

CHORUS:
must be examined

JUDITH:
must be examined

CRONE:
– examined, examined –

MAN: *taking the bomb back from Judith and putting it on her desk*
– as carefully as a bomb's fuse and circuit

CRONE:
– fuse and circuit –

MAN:
with the tender skill a surgeon uses
cutting live flesh

CRONE: *gloatingly – the 'Stone-Age self' speaking*
– live flesh, live flesh –

MAN:
to open up a heart

CHORUS, JUDITH AND MAN: *chanting in unison*
– a heart, a heart, a heart –

Man takes heart from Crone and puts it next to the bomb on Judith's desk.

344

CRONE:
Don't hurt my heart! *same conditioned response to word 'heart'*

CHORUS:
A test, a test,
the story is a test,
and if you pass the test,
each wish is granted –

JUDITH: *triumphant becaues she can express her wish*
I want to break the mould.
I want to tell a different story.

MAN:
My dear, my dear, my child.

JUDITH:
Have you hurt yourself?
They address each other, trying out different roles in a liberated, playful way – 'telling a different story'.

CHORUS: *Repeating her last line, carrying on through the interruptions, like a schoolteacher.*
Each wish is granted –
to change the definitions
and let the variations flourish –

JUDITH: *excited by this clear statement*
to change the definitions –
sits down at her desk & starts writing, as if making notes

CHORUS: *as if intoning a list*
of feminine
and masculine
son and mother

CRONE & JUDITH: *They do not sing in unison but in different tones of voice: Crone as if the words are Holy Writ,*

345

*Judith as if considering their meaning & whether she agrees
with them.*
   – son and mother –

CHORUS:
   love and duty

CRONE & JUDITH: *Judith keeps her head down, writing*
   – love and duty –

CHORUS:
   and that final one, 'The End',

JUDITH: *looks up from her work triumphantly*
   I can make the story
   different every time!

MAN:
   Have you hurt yourself, have you hurt yourself?

JUDITH:
   My dear, my dearest child?
*They are trying the lines in yet another way, like a game.
Judith's tone: does she want him to be her child?*

CRONE: *These are the vital instructions to Judith from the
deepest part of her being. She hears 'that special note' for the
first time. The rite de pasage has been enacted.*
   Don't throw the bomb.
   Don't hurt yourself.

JUDITH AND CHORUS: *In same positions as at beginning –
Judith seated at her desk, Chorus looking over her shoulder.*
   But we can break the mould
   and change the images,
   and we can tell the story –

CHORUS: *stepping away from Judith as the others come
near her*
   It started in Europe.

346

JUDITH & CRONE & MAN:
  – the story, story, story –

CHORUS:
  It spread like radiation.

JUDITH & CRONE & MAN:
  – the story, story, story –

CHORUS:
  There's no immunity to images.

JUDITH & CRONE & MAN:
  – tell the story
  different every time.